A WAY OF LIFE

John 6:40—"And this is the will of Him who sent Me, that everyone who sees the Son and believes in Him may have everlasting life…"

Awakening the Force Within

NANCY WILLIAMS

Nancy Williams
P.O. Box 4373
Mission Viejo, CA 96291
Or
Contact the author at NancyWilliams.org

A Way of Life
Awakening The Force Within
http://www.NancyWilliams.org
All Rights Reserved by Nancy Williams.

ISBN: 1523807105
ISBN-13: 9781523807109

Library of Congress Control Number: 2016901756
CreateSpace Independent Publishing Platform
North Charleston, South Carolina

PRINTED IN THE UNITED STATES OF AMERICA

To order additional copies of this resource
Visit: NancyWilliams.org, Barnes and Nobe & Amazon
Available also by ebook

ABOUT THE AUTHOR

My HEART'S CRY is one of freedom and abundance for you, who read this. I was born and raised in the Panama Canal Zone, and accepted Jesus Christ as my Lord and Savior between the ages of 10-13. While I was being raised, God called me off by myself to spend time with Him, reading His Word by the sparkling blue, Caribbean water. He was my teacher and even with that, many mistakes did I make! When I was 17, He called me to be a Registered Nurse and it was during one of my areas of work that an earlier edition of this book was born.

I married at 22 to an unbeliever, was divorced at 30, and went through what I call baptism by fire during my first marriage. God had me clean up all that I was doing that was not loving or supporting my marriage, regardless of what my ex-husband was or was not doing. Doing what is right because it is right, is the right thing to do though it's not easy. Especially when my own needs were not being met! The earlier edition of this book was completed during this season of life and I began teaching God's principles of living a victorious life in the community for many years.

During the writing process, there were many times that I stopped as I did not know what the next step was. I sought the Lord and He answered me, and only then did I move on and continued this journey. One summer, I remember sitting at my desk while the sun was shining brightly on the deep colored greenery outside my window. I looked at everyone playing while I sat working with the sun playing on the leaves. I chose to not get up and play, because above all else, my hearts cry is one of freedom and abundance for you who read this. Even then, I knew that to create something great requires sacrifice and I knew that I would either get my reward later, or maybe never. The reward did not matter. What was and still is important, is that I finish the work I promised God I would and was called to do.

I have since remarried, have a wonderful family, and look forward to more of God's blessings in my life as I give to others! May you ask Him for your way and follow it. Therein is fulfillment and blessings galore. Why else should we be here but to live out what was ordained for each of us from the beginning of the world? That is why this work was written. That is why this work was written for you.

With blessings always,

Nancy Williams

DEDICATION

To those who read this:

This is dedicated to you, in the hopes that through this book you will find a deeper meaning in your walk with Christ. My hope is that a living Christianity will be yours — that you are able to feel how much you are loved; that you are able to see more clearly how the Bible applies to you; and that you will then embrace and incorporate these principles into your way of being and living.

I want to thank and acknowledge my loving husband, Jaycee, and daughter, Natalie, for lovingly and graciously supporting me as I took time away to complete this labor of love.

How to Use The Following Chapters

BRINGING SINFUL PATTERNS to the surface and dealing with them according to God's principles will restore our path in life and repair the breech that separates us from others and from God, to borrow from Isaiah 58:12. Individuals who have gone through this book have found God's living Force and stated that they have been able to trust God and look with honesty on their lives.

God calls us to live a principled life and as we incorporate His principles found in this book in our lives, His living Force will flow. This book emphasizes God's principles as found in the Bible as the only source of living. As God created the world and set-up universal principles by which it operates, relational principles are found in this creation. Since He set it all up, He and His principles are the source of life and as we incorporate them, our lives will work. Therefore, memorize some of the given scriptures as the Holy Spirit will bring them to your remembrance in time of need. God's Word will not return void (Isaiah 55:11), and you will be affected by memorizing His Word even if you do not feel that an impact was immediately made. In each chapter, answer the questions to the best of your ability and you will be amazed at what starts happening within you!

If going through A Way of Life in a group setting, the facilitator may decide to share a short weekly teaching which provides the biblical foundation for the principle/s being reviewed, such as confession or repentance. The main group could then be divided into groups with a group facilitator present to promote sharing what God is doing in each other's lives, what the chapter review has brought to light, and any hindrance in depending on God. The main facilitator may bring the whole group back together at the end for sharing and prayer.

Additional supportive subjects such as goal setting, writing a life philosophy, and effective communication tools are found in the appendix at the back of this book.

And now, let us continue with discovering how to awaken God's Force within us!

CONTENTS

Introduction xi

    The Force xi

Preface xiii

    What does it mean to Be? xiii

No Pain, No Gain xv

Life Philosophy xvii

Goals and Objectives xix

Chapter 1   The Covenant and The Force · 1

Chapter 2   Responding to The Force · 15

Chapter 3   Letting Go of Control to The Force · · · · · · · · · · · · · · 23

Chapter 4   Taking Stock with The Force · · · · · · · · · · · · · · · · · · · 31

Chapter 5   Confession in The Light of The Force · · · · · · · · · · · · 43

Chapter 6   Willingness to Work with The Force · · · · · · · · · · · · · 47

Chapter 7   Humility Before The Force · 55

Chapter 8   True Forgiveness with the Support of The Force · · · · 61

Chapter 9   Reconcile with the Support of The Force · · · · · · · · · · 67

Chapter 10 Honesty to Yourself and to The Force · · · · · · · · · · · 71

Chapter 11 Silence and Submission to The Force · · · · · · · · · · · · 81

             The Flow · 84

Chapter 12 Sharing The Force with Others · · · · · · · · · · · · · · · · 87

          Suggested Reading List · 93

          Appendix · 95

▲▲▲

INTRODUCTION

THE FORCE

IN THE STAR Wars saga, the war against good and evil is extremely evident. On one side is the "good" side, called the force. On the other side is the "dark" side, which is evil. There is a call on the dark side to all who will hear to succumb to the pull of power, anger, death, and destruction. The evil force is so strong that it separates families, friends, and even those in power.

In the movie, the good force is portrayed as being a counselor; one who guides, leads to knowledge, and gives power to do and stand for good. This force is also portrayed as one who comes alongside you. This is very similar though pales when compared to God, in the person of the Holy Spirit, who is a counselor, knowledge and wisdom giver, and who can be *in you* and come alongside you if you ask Him to! Just to be clear, in this book the Force refers to God's Holy Spirit and not the good side of the force depicted in the movies. The dark side depicted in the movies is the force of evil in the world, which is still present today.

So, on one side is the force of good and the other, the force of evil. Even the light sabers portray this with the evil color being red and the good color being a light whitish color. The pitting of good against evil is as old as the ages and it still sells. Have you asked yourself, why?

It sells because we as humans want good to triumph over evil, which gives us hope and makes us feel good when we see good triumph. We hope that our fellow human beings and even ourselves can overcome the evil pull and do good. Be good.

This book serves to uncover what force holds everything together, which was even talked about in one of the Star Wars episodes, and to bring to light that there are light and dark forces at work around us—ALL the time. We all know about the evil force that pulls us to do wrong things and wants to keep us beaten down. This book will walk you through how to awaken the (good) godly force within you and how to be an overcomer, as you move to live out what was ordained for you from the beginning of time. This book will show how God's holy Force (His Holy Spirit) can talk to you, give you advance knowledge, lead and guide you into all truth, and warn you of danger, to list a few of the works He does! This book is not for those who like the dark side and want to stay hidden but is for all others. If you are reading this, this book is for you.

PREFACE

WHAT DOES IT MEAN TO BE?

As humans and as Christians, we hear well-meaning messages about loving one another, treating each other with compassion, kindness, and doing what's right. And yet, this message misses the mark. We attempt to put on these character traits rather than Be them and then wonder why we don't get the results we want in our lives. Loving, authentic Christianity is not our witness. So why is this? It's because we are not being authentic or coming from the core of who we were created to be. We were created to Be love. Our English sentence structure sums up the contrast exceptionally well in regards to this dilemma and I will include Jesus in these two sentences, as He is our example.

1. Jesus was and is love.
2. Jesus loved.

The first sentence shows the state of being that Jesus was and is always in. The second sentence demonstrates the result of the first sentence. Jesus came from an unconditional, divine state of being so He could then love. He was love on the inside first. Then, and only then, could He manifest in power, effect, and results. He chose to Be this, and is this.

So what does this tell us about how we are to live and Be? It's by choice. It's by choice, intention, and commitment, empowered by His Holy Spirit. It's a state of being, powered by choice. When we are, we are authentic. Whether or not our state of being is positive or negative, it is extremely powerful.

So the bottom line issue is, what state of being do we most live in and what can we do to change where we live? Are we closed, reserved, rigid, irritated, legalistic, rushed, numb, or angry? How about open, calm, joyful, authentic, honest, or loving? To follow Jesus' example, we are to notice moment by moment what state of being we are in. If this state of being does not authentically love, we get to choose to move into the example Jesus gave us of unconditional, authentic love. It is in this state that the abundant life can flow through us to others and this life can be true, pure, and lovely. When we **are** unconditional love, we are truly free.

Free to fly to the music of His joy,
Free to feel the waves tumble us in playfulness,
Free Choice—
The way it is meant to be.

▲ ▲ ▲

No Pain, No Gain

"No pain, No gain".
These are the words the athletes sing
As they work their muscles to the sting.

"It hurts, it hurts," they cry
As the burning goes deeper and deeper in their thigh.

And yet they push on to never-ending fights,
Knowing that without this pain, they would never reach the heights.

And so I say to you — you who so resist your pain —
Work it to the bone and do not deter,
For with your pain, you will gain.

—WHAT WE RESIST, PERSISTS—

▲ ▲ ▲

LIFE PHILOSOPHY

BASED ON ROMANS 3:23, where God says that all have sinned and fall short of the glory of God, it is this book's premise that all of us are in need of healing. We believe it is through sin, starting with Adam and Eve and passed down from generation to generation, that dysfunctional patterns began. It is sin that separates us from God, says Isaiah 59:2.

It is our goal to facilitate:

    1st — Looking at ourselves honestly.
    2nd — Accepting God's grace, love, and truth so that
    3rd — We can be set free from our sin.

We propose to do this by using God's Word and following His way.

We believe the fruit of this will be:

    1st — An intimate relationship with God the Father, God the Son, and God the Holy Spirit, so that
    2nd — The abundant life force from God will be ours as we live and grow in this dynamic relationship.

Goals and Objectives

- For you to become aware of your perceptions of God.
- For you to find out what God says He is like.
- For you to take your incongruent perceptions of God to Him.
- An increased desire to ask Him to change you.
- That you begin to trust Him more.

By the end of this book, you will be able to:

- Have more intimacy with God and your fellow man.
- Begin to understand God's purpose for you.
- Identify how to be free from the bondage of sin.
- Find salvation (if not truly born again but merely religious).
- Look to the future with a heart full of hope.
- Have an increased understanding of the Holy Spirit, God's holy Force.
- Trust God and your fellow man to a greater degree.
- Identify manipulative vs. truthful communication patterns.

1

THE COVENANT AND THE FORCE

God's Principles: Covenant, Sin, Grace, and Mercy

COVENANT

A COVENANT RELATIONSHIP with God and how you understand this relationship is vital to receiving the Force from God and trusting Him. Read the following while seeking to allow the Holy Spirit (God's holy Force) to speak and touch you in this area of your life.

Are you able to recognize that the Lord is the Lord of the universe and all that is in it? What is your understanding of His covenant towards you? As you come to see and know His covenant towards you, my hope is that trust can grow with the subsequent laying of yourself down before Him as you come to appreciate His everlasting guidance (holy Force) and provision for you.

Webster defines covenant as "a formal, solemn, and binding agreement; a written agreement between two parties, especially for the performance of some action." The Bible describes three main covenants: the Abrahamic, the Old Covenant, and the New Covenant. In the covenant with Abraham, God promised that through Abraham and his descendants, all the world would be blessed (Genesis 12-15). Circumcision was given as a sign for every male child to show that God would be their God. They became a set-apart people, a peculiar people into the beginnings of a community of true worshipers of God. God gave the land of Canaan to Abraham, Isaac, and then Jacob (Genesis 35:12). He permitted no man to do them wrong as they went from one nation to another, saying, "Do not touch My anointed ones, and do My prophets no harm" (1 Chronicles 16:22). God was promising to protect and guide this special community. Abraham "believed God and it was accounted to him for righteousness", which is why he is called the father of the faithful (Galatians 3:6-7). Likewise, God calls us to believe Him and be His people.

The Old Covenant was a promise from God to those who left Egypt and were being led by Him to the Promised Land. To Moses and the children of Israel, God said in Exodus 19:5-6, "If you will indeed obey My voice and keep My covenant, then you shall be a special treasure to Me above all people; for all the earth is Mine. And you shall be to Me a kingdom of priests and a holy nation." T.B. Maston, in his book Biblical Ethics, states that, "God is always the initiator of the covenant; it is not a contract between two people of equal or near-equal standing. It is unilateral. GOD ALONE states the conditions of the covenant; the people could not negotiate with God regarding the covenant nor change its conditions. They could either accept or reject it. Once accepted, they could not annul it, but could violate its conditions. God alone had the power to dissolve the covenant, a power He never used. He is revealed not only as a covenant-giving but also as a covenant-keeping God." The Ten Commandments were then given to Moses for the people of God in Exodus 20, as their part in the covenant relationship. As God promises to lead, guide, and protect His people, He also requires His people to obey His Word. The covenant to do as

God commanded was accepted verbally by Israel in Exodus 19 and ratified by a blood sacrifice in Exodus 24 after the specific behavior obligations for God's people (the Ten Commandments) were laid down in stone.

Throughout the exodus from Egypt, God directed His people by a pillar of cloud by day and a pillar of fire by night and provided for their thirst, hunger, and protection (Exodus 13-17). Similarly, God desires to guide and provide for His people today. The Old Testament continually pointed to the coming Messiah, the King of kings and Lord of lords. Jesus, in the New Covenant, came to fulfill what had been proclaimed. Again, God had a plan which was and is to continue to gather a people to Himself. But something happened before the Abrahamic and Old Covenants even existed.

In the beginning, God created the heavens and the earth and all that was in them. He created Adam and Eve and talked and walked with them in a special, holy, and right relationship. They were given the command to take care of the earth and have dominion over it. Everything lived in harmony as there was a perfect union between God, man, and the world He had made. In the Garden of Eden, Satan, whose original name was Lucifer and who had been a powerful angel in heaven, had previously been thrown from heaven as he wanted power and to be above God. A third of the angels sided with him and were thrown to the earth with him. Satan's goal is to keep as many people away from God and going towards a path of death and destruction--the dark side. Therefore, in the Garden of Eden Satan tempted Adam and Eve to doubt God and go their own way, which they did. At their turning away from the one thing God asked them not to do (eat of one particular tree's fruit), disobedience and sin entered the world and man fell from having a right relationship with God and from having dominion over the earth. The decay started and there was division rather than harmony or unity. The evil (dark) force now had dominion over the earth but Jesus came to restore this relationship back to the way it was intended in Genesis. He did this by shedding His blood on the cross to pay for our disobedience to His ways. Prior to Jesus' death, the people of God shed blood for the forgiveness of their sins with animal sacrifice. Jesus came so that we do not have to pay the price of spiritual death (eternal separation from God) for our sins nor shed animal blood. He shed His blood for us and rose from the dead, so that we may live. He opened the way to God through His death and resurrection, saying, "I am the way, the truth, and the life. No one comes to the Father except through Me" (John 14:6). Because of Christ's mercy, we who believe have been forgiven and will not receive the judgment due us. Jesus conquered Satan, the power of death, the power of our flesh, and the power of sin over us with His death and resurrection. In Him, we are victors. Satan, our flesh, and sin have no power over us that we do not allow. Ephesians 6 lists the protective armor God provides for every Christian.

Jesus came also to write His Word not on stone, as in the Old Covenant, but on the tablets of our hearts (2 Corinthians 3:3). As we receive and accept the work that Jesus did on the cross for us, He gives us Himself in the Person of the Holy Spirit to "teach you all things" (John 14:26) as well as "guide you into all truth; for He will not speak on His own authority, but whatever He hears He will speak; and He will tell you things to come" (John 16:13). This Holy Spirit is God's holy Force, given to indwell us to lead and guide us if we accept the fact that Jesus paid the penalty of our sins by dying on the cross as a living sacrifice. Jesus won the battle over Satan (dark side) through His death and resurrection and has given you all the tools necessary to make disciples of all nations (Matthew 28:19). The battle armor of Ephesians 6 helps us take back the land that has been usurped by Satan, the world, and our flesh. We can do it because Jesus said, "Lo, I am with you always, even to the end of the age" (Matthew 28:20).

Are we sons of Abraham who believe what God says? Are we watchful for the birds of prey (Satan, our flesh, and the world) that will come to wreak havoc with our belief? They seek to attack our emotions and our minds through depression and doubt. Why do these birds of prey come? Because, AS WE BELIEVE GOD AND WHAT HE SAYS, THIS IS THE KEY TO THE KINGDOM BEING ESTABLISHED HERE ON EARTH AS IT IS IN HEAVEN. SATAN (the dark side) DOESN'T WANT THAT TO HAPPEN! When we pray to receive Christ (the righteous, holy, light side) as our personal savior, God gives us a permanent, covenantal relationship. This covenant is a sacred, holy, reverent bond.

What does our side of the covenant consist of? Jesus sacrificed Himself in obedience to God, the Father. Have we sacrificed ourselves in obedience to God's Word? Romans12:1 calls us to be a "living sacrifice" — to die to self, I, and me, which is contrary to our American society. When we live for ourselves, we try to meet our needs through control, manipulation, and guilt, which quench love. We were made in the image of God and God is love. To really live, we get to die to ourselves so that God's love can reign in us. Where are we in our decision for God? Have we entered into a relationship with Jesus by accepting Him only and by making a sacrifice of our will to His will? Are we very much alive and still kicking? Jesus promises, "He who loses his life for My sake will find it" (Matthew 10:39).

There are conditions to God's many promises that we are responsible to fulfill. Do we ask for the promises but forget about the conditions? For instance, God promises us in James 4:7 that the devil will flee from us. The conditions stated are that we are to submit ourselves to God and resist the devil — then and only then does the promise come that the devil will flee from us. Romans 8:28 states that "all things work together for good to those who love God, to those who are the called according to His purpose," which is fellowship with Him and obedience to His commands. A non-believer cannot stand on this promise of God, "….that all things work together for good." As we cease rebelling and do the conditions stated in God's Word, our lives become peaceful and more harmonious. It is the way we are meant to live for God knows what works and what doesn't!

If we want Him to speak to us, we get to choose to come to Him as little children in simple faith, looking for His will to be worked in our lives and He will meet us. He promises us that, through the Person and work of the Holy Spirit (John 14:26) as well as through the Person of Christ, who said, "Ask, and it will be given to you; seek, and you will find; knock, and it will be opened to you" (Matthew 7:7).

Have you doubted that God directs today and are you looking for His will in your life? Look at Acts, chapter 13 where Barnabas and Saul were sent out in a particular direction by the injunction of God's holy Force, the Holy Spirit. This same Spirit is available to lead us into all truth and to show us things to come (John 16:13). An absolutely surrendered will brings clarity to our mind in the discernment of God's will as revealed by His Spirit.

The Holy Spirit is the Third Person of our Triune God. He has distinctive characteristics of personality: knowledge (1 Corinthians 2:10-11), will (1 Corinthians 12:11), mind (Romans 8:27), love (Romans 15:30), goodness (Nehemiah 9:20), and grief (Ephesians 4:30). R.A. Torrey portrays that The Holy Spirit is not a blind, impersonal influence or power that comes into our lives to illuminate, sanctify, and empower us. He is a holy Person who comes to dwell in our hearts. One who knows fully every act we perform, every word we speak, every thought we entertain that is allowed to pass through our minds. If there is anything in thought, word, or action that is impure, unholy, unkind, selfish, mean, petty or untrue, this infinitely Holy One is deeply grieved by it. What is our relationship with this Holy One? It has been my experience that as I have sincerely asked my Father to reveal His truth to me and the path He has ordained for me, He does so through the Person of the Holy Spirit. He promises to! I can rest and wait for His Word to me. When I hear, then I can run. Why run when I don't know where I am going? Then, I would have run in vain. This Holy Spirit, the third Person of the trinity, is God's holy Force that penetrates and guides us into living out the abundant life God has created and ordained for each of us.

Do you see that God is calling a special people to Himself — a holy people — a holy nation? Do you see that God has won the battle? That Satan has already been defeated? That God has always had a plan to draw His creations unto Himself? That He promises always to be there for you to guide and to protect, for only that which He allows can touch you? That He has given you His own Spirit with which to go forth and make disciples of all nations? That if you are God's, you are a Force Warrior! That you are a part of an army in a war fighting for the land given to us that Satan has ravaged?

I have shown the continual promise of God to a people (you) who set themselves apart for Him and Him alone. He wants a special, peculiar people, and indeed, this is a peculiar way but it is the only way. Can you accept and believe? Can you appropriate all that was given to you at the death and resurrection of Jesus? I hope that A Way of Life will help you appropriate all that God has given you and that increased trust in Him happens in you.

▲ ▲ ▲

THE LAW

The law can be defined as that which proceeds from the mouth of God (God's Word) to outline the way we are to live. There are several categories of God's law and one category is the Law of Moses, which includes the Ten Commandments. The conditions that go along with some of God's stated promises in His Word is another category. Overall, however, the primary purpose of the law is to convict man of his sin. It is a standard to be met. It serves to convince men of their natural inability to keep the law perfectly, which is a moral rather than an intellectual or physical issue. It points out the need of some other means or method of freedom from the inherent guilt that stems from our inability to keep God's law. The law also promotes righteousness and restrains wickedness (sin).

SIN

The Greek word translated "sin" (hamartia) means "missing the mark." It is an archer's term, picturing an arrow that flies toward the target but falls short. Sin is principally defined as anything contrary to the law of God, for 1 John 3:4 declares, "sin is lawlessness." In Scripture, sin is viewed first and foremost in relation to God and the law and then to our neighbor. Just as there is an absolute with good, so is there an absolute with sin. It is either sin or not sin. Sin stems from the heart, so does not consist of outward acts alone. Heart attitudes as well as sinful habits eventually lead us to sinful deeds. Therefore, evil thoughts, affections, and intents of the heart are to be regarded as sinful. ANY SINFUL THOUGHT OR DEED IS FIRST A SIN AGAINST THE CREATOR OF THE UNIVERSE — GOD. The result is true guilt before our Maker, making us liable for punishment, and causing death within us (Romans 6:23).

GRACE

By the law of God, we know sin. By sin, we are guilty. Grace then, is the unearned love of God toward us. The Greek word most often translated "grace" in the New Testament (Charis) is defined as favor, acceptance, a kindness granted, and a favor done without expectation of return. It is an absolutely free gift of the loving-kindness of God to us, finding its only motive in the bounty and free heartedness of the Giver. It is completely unearned and unmerited favor. The operation of God's Holy Spirit (His Force) that enables us to walk God's way of life with favor, is one of His greatest graces.

For God's grace to provide healing from our sin we must first truly want help. To get to this point we must come to some recognition that our lives are not working and empty. Our society does not program us to acknowledge nor accept the fact that we cannot, "on our own", live lovingly. We are programmed from day one to be competitive, proud of our accomplishments, look good, and not let others control us, but stay in control of ourselves. This outward appearance is what we use to give ourselves worth as individuals. If that is our core, we are not in touch with who we are inside and are covered in denial, which makes us lonely and unable to connect with others. Jesus said, "Whoever desires to save his life will lose it, but whoever loses his life for My sake will find it" (Matthew 16:25). We are able to find ourselves when we relinquish control to the Almighty, who made us, the heavens, and the earth. We who think we are in control are not. It is only when we trust our creator that we are set free from the chains that bind us and can find who we were created to be. We can find our true selves.

MERCY

Grace and mercy are closely related. God's mercy means that He will not put on us the judgment or consequences of our sin that we deserve. The misery of sin will be removed by God's mercy as long as the guilt and power of sin are removed through God's grace first. We, in turn, can be merciful to others as God has been merciful to us.

The following questions are designed to probe your perceptions, thought processes, and behaviors — all to support your growth forward into freedom and support the awakening of the Force in you.

As I look at life, my understanding of God's law is:_____

_____

My understanding of sin is:_____

_____

The Holy Spirit throughout your life will bring different sins to your attention for the purpose of:

- Working with you to rid yourself of them.
- Being in a closer relationship to your Heavenly Father.

Many times, however, we don't want to look or work with God's Force, the Holy Spirit.

The ways in which I have denied looking at myself include:_____

_____

The outstanding sin or sins in my life right now are: _____

_____

When I hear of God's grace, I understand this to be: _____

_____

What message have you received from society or your parents relating to your worth as a person? What is/or was important to them regarding the way others looked at them or your family?

_____

What area of your life has been the most unmanageable? _____

_____

How have you tried to manage your life in the past? _____

_____

What behaviors do you find yourself employing to manage your life? _____

_____

What has been the consequences of those behaviors? _____

_____

Why shouldn't I depend upon myself for my life? (Romans 7:18—"I know that in me [this is, in my flesh] nothing good dwells; for to will is present with me, but how to perform what is good I do not find.")

_____

In what way does God say that I am powerless, in Romans 7:15? "For what I am doing, I do not understand. For what I will to do, that I do not practice; but what I hate, that I do."

_____

What fears do you have about looking at your true self? _____

_____

What does God say about the peace that He gives to you, in John 14:37? "Peace I leave with you, My peace I give to you; not as the world gives do I give to you. Let not your heart be troubled, neither let it be afraid."_____

_____

What is your belief about God's covenant relationship with you?

_____

What doubts do you have that He made this covenant with you?

_____

What did the shedding of Jesus' blood on the cross do for you?

_____

In your heart of hearts, do you believe it is enough to cover all? _____

_____

What does Jesus' blood not cover for you? _____

_____

▲ ▲ ▲

A LOOK AT MY FAMILY

The following exercise is to bring forth the truth about our families of origin, in order that we may be healed. Hiding or sweeping issues under the rug never takes care of the root cause, which we are attempting to find and bring healing to. The list below and following definitions, is taken from The Family by John Bradshaw (Health Communications, Inc. 1988), and is used with permission from the author. The definition of each term is on subsequent pages.

Directions: Use the next pages and read about each item on the following list and what it means. If the definition pertains to you, circle the letter below and continue on to the next letter and the corresponding definition.

A   Abandonment Issues.
D   Delusion and Denial
U   Undifferentiated Ego Mass
L   Loneliness and Isolation
T   Thought Disorders

C   Control Madness
H   Hyper-vigilant and High Level Anxiety
I   Internalized Shame
L   Lack of Boundaries
D   Disabled Will
R   Reactive and Re-enacting
E   Equifinality
N   Numbed Out

O   Offender with or without Offender Status
F   Fixated Personality

D   Dissociated Responses
Y   Yearning for Parental Warmth and Approval
S   Secrets
F   Faulty Communication Style
U   Under-involved
N   Neglect of Developmental Dependency Needs
C   Compulsive/Addictive
T   Trance
I   Intimacy Problems
O   Over-involved
N   Narcissistically Deprived
A   Abuse Victim
L   Lack of Coping Skills (under-learning)

F   False Self—confused Identity
A   Avoid Depression through Activity
M   Measured, Judgmental, and Perfectionist
I   Inhibited Trust
L   Loss of Your Own Reality
I   Inveterate Dreamer
E   Emotional Constraint
S   Spiritual Bankruptcy

A. ABANDONMENT ISSUES

One or both of your parents physically abandoned you. Or, they might have been physically present but not emotionally available to you. Someone physically, sexually, or emotionally violated you in your family. Your developmental dependency needs were neglected. You were enmeshed in your parents' neediness or in the needs of your family system. You stay in relationships far beyond what is healthy.

D. DELUSION AND DENIAL

You think you had a great childhood and that your family was the good old American Family.

U. UNDIFFERENTIATED EGO MASS

You carry feelings, desires, and secrets of other people in your family system.

L. LONELINESS AND ISOLATION

You have felt lonely all or most of your life. You feel isolated and different.

T. THOUGHT DISORDERS

You get preoccupied with generalities or details. You worry, ruminate, and obsess a lot. You stay in your head to avoid your feelings. You read about your problems rather than take action.

C. CONTROL MADNESS

You try to control yourself and everyone else. You feel extremely uncomfortable when you're out of control. You mask your efforts to control people and situations by "being helpful."

H. HYPERVIGILANT AND HIGH ANXIETY

You live on guard. You are easily startled. You panic easily.

I. INTERNALIZED SHAME

You feel flawed as a human being. You feel inadequate and hide behind a role or an addiction or character trait like control, blame, criticism, perfectionism, contempt, power, and rage.

L. LACK OF BOUNDARIES

You don't know where you end and others begin — physically, emotionally, intellectually, or spiritually. You don't know what you really stand for.

D. DISABLED WILL

You are willful. You try to control other people. You are grandiose. With you it's all or nothing.

R. REACTIVE AND RE-ENACTING

You react easily. You feel things that are not related to what is happening. You feel things more intensely than the event calls for. You find yourself repeating patterns over and over.

E. EQUIFINALITY

No matter where you begin, your life seems to end at the same place.

N. NUMBED OUT
You don't feel your feelings. You don't know what you feel. You don't know how to express what you feel.

O. OFFENDER WITH OR WITHOUT OFFENDER STATUS
You offend people, or you play that role occasionally.

F. FIXATED PERSONALITY
You are an adult, but your emotional age is very young. You look like an adult, but feel very childlike and needy. You feel like the lifeguard on a crowded beach, but you don't know how to swim. (You're in charge but you don't know what to do)

D. DISSOCIATED RESPONSES
You have no memories of painful events of your childhood; you have a split personality; you depersonalize; can't remember people's names, even people you were with only two years ago. You are out of touch with your body and your feelings.

Y. YEARN FOR PARENTAL WARMTH AND APPROVAL — YOU SEEK IT IN OTHER RELATIONSHIPS
You still try to gain your parents' approval. You yearn for the perfect relationship. You have an exaggerated need for others' approval. You fear offending others. You find emotionally unavailable partners (just like your parents were), whom you try to make love you. You will go to almost any lengths to care and help your partner. Almost nothing is too much trouble. Having had little nurturing yourself, you find people who need nurturing and take care of them.

S. SECRETS
You carry lots of secrets from your family of origin. You've never talked to anyone about how bad it was in your family, and you carry lots of secrets about your own life. You also carry lots of sexual secrets you would not want to tell anyone.

F. FAULTY COMMUNICATION
You have had trouble communicating in every relationship you've been in. No one seems to understand what you say. You feel confused when communicating with others. When talking to your parents, no matter how good your intentions are to be sane and clear, the results are conflicted and confused.

U. UNDER-INVOLVED
You stand on the sidelines of life, wishing you were a participant. You don't know how to initiate a relationship, a conversation, or an activity. You are withdrawn and would rather bear the pangs of being alone than risk interaction. You are not spontaneous. You allow yourself very little excitement or fun.

N. NEGLECT OF DEVELOPMENTAL DEPENDENCY NEEDS
You have a hole in the cup of your psyche. You never seem to be satisfied. No matter how much you anticipate something, soon after it is over, you feel restless and unsatisfied. You are childish and feel like a child most of the time. You cry when someone says really beautiful things about you. You feel like you don't really belong wherever you are.

C. COMPULSIVE/ADDICTIVE
You have been or are now in an active compulsive addictive behavior.

T. TRANCE
You are fantasy bonded and still idealize your parents, continuing to play the role you played in your family system. Nothing has really changed in your family of origin: the same dialogue, the same fights, and the same gossip. Your marriage or your relationship is like that of your parents.

I. INTIMACY PROBLEMS
You have trouble in relationships. You have been married more than twice, choosing partners who embody the same emotional patterns of your primary caretakers. You are attracted to seductive, psychopathic partners; you are not attracted to partners who are kind, stable, reliable, and interested in you. You find nice men and women boring. When you start getting too close, you leave a relationship. You confuse closeness with compliance; intimacy with fusion.

O. OVER-INVOLVED
You are drawn to people who are needy. You confuse love with pity. You are drawn to people who have problems you can get involved in fixing. You are drawn toward people and situations that are chaotic, uncertain, and emotionally painful.

N. NARCISSISTICALLY DEPRIVED
You feel empty and childishly helpless inside. You compensate with addiction to such things as chemicals, food, prestige, money, possessions, heroism, sex, power, or violence as a way of feeling important and worthwhile.

A. ABUSE VICTIM
You were physically, emotionally, or sexually abused as a child. You have become a victim in life and play that role in all areas of your life. You feel hopeless about changing anything. Or, you were abused and have become an offender. You identified with the abusing parent or caretaker and act just like he or she did.

L. LACK OF COPING SKILLS (UNDER-LEARNING)
You never learned how to do many things necessary for a fully functional life. Your methods of problem solving do not work, but you continue to use the same ones over and over. You learned ways of caring for your wounds that, in fact, perpetuated them. You have no real knowledge of what is normal. Your bottom-line tolerance is quite abnormal.

F. FALSE SELF — CONFUSED IDENTITY
Your self-worth depends on your partner's success or failure. When you're not in a relationship, you feel an inner void. You feel responsible for making your partner happy. You take care of people to give yourself an identity. You wear masks, calculate, manipulate and play games. You act out rigid family or sex roles. When your partner has a stomachache, you take Pepto-Bismol!

A. AVOID DEPRESSION THROUGH ACTIVITY
You get involved in unstable relationships. The more you are physically and mentally active, the more you can avoid your depression.

M. MEASURED, JUDGMENTAL, AND PERFECTIONIST
You have unrealistic expectations of yourself and others. You are rigid and inflexible, overly judgmental of yourself and others. You are stuck in your attitudes and behavior, even though it hurts to live the way you do.

I. INHIBITED TRUST
You really don't trust anyone, including your own feelings, perceptions, and judgments.

L. LOSS OF YOUR OWN REALITY — DAMAGED AND WEAK BOUNDARIES
You take more than 50 percent for the responsibility, guilt, and blame for whatever happens in a relationship. You know what others feel or need before you know your own feelings and needs. Rather than take any risk of abandonment, you have withdrawn and refuse to get involved. You regard any change in the status quo of a relationship as a threat. You feel embarrassed by what others do and take inappropriate responsibility for their behavior.

I. INVETERATE DREAMER
You are more in touch with your dreams of how things could be, rather than with the reality of your life and situation. You live according to an ideal image of yourself, having a grandiose and exaggerated notion of yourself. You fantasize, catastrophize, and exaggerate the seriousness of decisions and events.

E. EMOTIONAL CONSTRAINT (WITH OR WITHOUT DRAMATIC OUTBURST)
You believe that controlling your emotions is a way to control your life. You attempt to manage your life and your emotions. You have dramatic inappropriate outbursts of emotions that have been repressed for long periods of time. For example, you yell at your children after holding in your anger all day at work. You compulsively expose your emotions. You go to great lengths to verbalize every feeling as soon as it enters your awareness. You do this so that you won't have to feel them for very long.

S. SPIRITUAL BANKRUPTCY
You believe that your worth and happiness lies outside yourself. You have no awareness of your inner life since you spend all your energy avoiding your shame-based inner self.

All the families we have examined so far have certain structural similarities:

- A dominant dysfunction causes a threat to which all other family members respond. The adaptations to the threat cause the system to close up in a frozen and rigid pattern.
- The frozen pattern is maintained by each member playing one or more rigid roles.
- There is a high level of anxiety and confusion.
- All members are shame-based and shame is the organizing principle of all dysfunctional families.
- The more the system tries to change, the more it stays the same.

Think about what you just circled and then answer the following questions.

What issues from the list stand out the most for you right now?

_____

_____

What do you see differently about your family of origin now than before reading this material?

_____

_____

In what areas of your life do you have trouble setting boundaries?

_____

_____

At what emotional age do you see yourself?

_____

Scripture to memorize: Romans 7:15 — "For what I am doing, I do not understand. For what I will to do, that I do not practice; but what I hate, that I do."

▲ ▲ ▲

2

RESPONDING TO THE FORCE

God's Principles: Surrender and Acceptance

SURRENDER

HEBREWS 13:8 TEACHES that "Jesus Christ is the same yesterday, today, and forever." He came to reconcile you to God and give you His spirit to make you whole. God is in control whether you believe that or not and if you do not acknowledge this truth, you likely will feel alone, isolated, and defeated. You may feel as if you can take care of yourself and that there is little need for support from other people or God. You may feel as if you are in control, which is a lost state and is not freedom.

Bondage stems from such attempts to control. You may also be living in a box where certain things are OK, others are not. The control over your actions likely comes from the outside and not the inside, which in incongruent. Congruence means that what is being done or said on the outside is what is happening on the inside.

In this box, you might do things because you have to, not necessarily because you want or choose to. You may be living with many shoulds, shouldn'ts and oughts tormenting you. That isn't how God means for you to live. Remember, Jesus said, "He who loses his life for My sake will find it" (Matthew 10:39).

What happens when you acknowledge that there are forces you cannot control and willingly yield control of your life to Christ?

- Fear could be felt—in the beginning it is scary to do this, for you will likely confront your past teaching and experiences regarding religion and God.
- You can start to feel openness.
- The ability to experience life and emotions begin—you can begin to experience your true self.
- Humility happens—you become teachable.
- False expectations of yourself begin to diminish and the box of unnecessary shoulds, and shouldn'ts crumbles.
- Spontaneity begins to happen.

How can you do this?

- Establish a growing (God establishes the initial relationship through salvation) relationship with Jesus Christ through faithful prayer, reading His Word, and getting together with other Christians.

- Remember that He is in control but has put You in charge! He gave you, through Adam, rulership, care, dominion, and oversight of what He gives you (see Genesis chapter 1:26-31 in the Bible).
- Talk to God about anything. Tell Him you are afraid to talk to Him, if that is the case.
- Listen, seek, and expect answers. Be quiet inside. The answers will come, but maybe not as you wish.

ACCEPTANCE

The above speaks of restoration as we accept God's way. God's principles here are surrender and acceptance. Surrender and acceptance to the fact that through the work of God's holy Force (Holy Spirit), He will change you to what God intended you to be, do, and then have before He even created you! He has a plan for your life! Many times you may believe that He wants to benefit and support others but do not believe that for yourself. He is asking you to begin to trust Him. He is asking you to believe that He loves you and has a plan and purpose for your life. Depending on your background, you may view God as an angry, controlling authority figure with His finger stretched out, condemning you. You may have anger toward Him because He did not do as you asked in a situation nor intervened as you wanted Him to. Maybe you are continuing to want things to go your way? God is asking you to surrender your will to His will for your life. Since He is the great I AM and has the universe in the palm of His hand, how much more does He know your needs?

God is your Creator and the Maker of the heavens and the earth. This doctrine of creation will not be discussed in detail here but I would like to encourage you to look at nature. Contemplate it. Look at how wonderfully made the human body is. Even with the abuse of high stress, drugs, alcohol, and food, our bodies fight to function harmoniously. The Creator of the universe exists and is the force that holds all things together. As you truly come to recognize the depth and breadth of Him, you will or are compelled to fall at His feet in surrender and acceptance. The Christian paradox is that **man is never completely free** until he **totally submits to God.**

Scripture to memorize: Zechariah 4:6 — "'Not by might, nor by power, but by My Spirit,' says the Lord of hosts."

List the thoughts that come to mind as you think of the word Father. Include what your relationship was with your father, as you were growing up:

_____

_____

Depending upon your past experiences, your response to God being your heavenly Father will either be pleasant, unpleasant, or a combination of the two. It is important to be aware of your response and to understand the perceptions you hold of Him. Many times you may see God as you see your own father, which is never an accurate picture. As you become aware of the misperceptions you might hold, you can then throw them away and embrace the truth about God.

Your perception of God can determine how readily you will come to Him and begin to trust Him, which will affect His working in your life to free you from the bondage you may be in. As you recognize your sin, go to Him in repentance, accept His forgiveness and your responsibility to work with Him in your change, and He will set you free. Jesus said, "If you abide in My Word, you are my disciples indeed. And you shall know the truth, and the truth shall make you free" (John 8:31-32).

DRAW A PICTURE OF WHAT YOU SEE AS GOD'S FACE WHEN YOU
THINK OF HIM LOOKING AT YOU

Terms to describe your view of God (e.g., harsh judge, forgiving, angry, loving): _____

_____

_____

I cannot look or come to God because:

_____

_____

When I consider that God is my Father, my reaction is:

_____

_____

I never had, or lost my faith in God because of the following experiences:

_____

_____

Romans 10:17 says, that "faith comes by hearing, and hearing by the Word of God." Faith is a free gift given by God (Ephesians 2:8-9). You can exercise your faith by obeying His Word no matter how you feel and lifting your fear/s to Him. As you risk, your trust in Him grows and you can lay more and more of your life down to His care. As you commune more and more with Him, you will begin to identify and experience His operation in your life. Your faith will increase and your sensitivity to His voice will grow.

In what way do you see God operating in your life right now?

_____

_____

We are a people of the "now" generation. We are not usually willing to wait, anticipate, or work through anything in our lives. Just know that implementing God's principles in your life is not usually an immediate occurrence so frustration may be a temptation. Realize that spiritual growth and healing is individual, so do not be discouraged if you do not feel that you are moving as fast as you want to.

What is your reaction to the time it takes for spiritual growth and healing? _____

_____

_____

In what areas do you see God restoring you to His original intention?

_____

_____

What does God say about fear and your mind, in 2 Timothy 1:7—"God has not given us a spirit of fear, but of power, and of love and of a sound mind?"

_____

_____

Allow this scripture to affect your emotions. How does it feel?

_____

_____

What does God say about times of trouble in Psalm 40:1-2—"I waited patiently for the Lord; and He inclined to me, and heard my cry. He also brought me up out of a horrible pit, out of the miry clay, and set my feet upon a rock, and established my steps?"

_____

_____

List any areas where you are having doubt in believing that God is your Father, that He wants the best for you, and that He has the power to save you and lift you up into the abundant life— see John 10:10.

_____

_____

God uses other individuals who have gone through similar experiences to help you see your own life clearer and to obtain some direction. He calls all of us to be a spiritual family who bears one another's burdens (Galatians 6:2).

What experiences have you had in the past of sharing yourself with others—either among your family of origin, friends, or church family?

_____

_____

How do you see this program filling your need for a spiritual family?

_____

_____

The following exercise will support the identification of what your perception is regarding your family of origin. The adaptability and attachment scales may bring to light ways of relating that have been passed down from generation to generation. There are no right answers or perfect families, so please be truthful with yourself!

FAMILY INVENTORY

From Forgiving Our Parents, Forgiving Ourselves by Dr. David Stoop and Dr. James Masteller (c) 1991 by Dr. David Stoop. Published by Servant Publications, Box 8617, Ann Arbor, Michigan 48107. Used with permission. Based on work done by David H. Olsen, reported in David H. Olsen, Hamilton I. McCubbin and Associates, Families: What Makes Them Work, (Newbury Park, CA: Sage Publishing, 1989).

For each of the following statements, write in a number according to the following scheme for your family:

1--almost never true
2--sometimes true
3--almost always true

_____ 1 Family members supported each other when they had problems.
_____ 2. Family members felt free to speak their minds.
_____ 3. It was easy to talk about almost anything with my family.
_____ 4. All family members participated in making family decisions.
_____ 5. Our family did a lot of things together.
_____ 6. In our family, children had a say in how they were disciplined.
_____ 7. Our family loved to be in the same room together.
_____ 8. Our family enjoyed discussing problems and solutions.
_____ 9. Each of us knew that our friends were also the family friends.
_____ 10. Everyone shared responsibilities in our family.
_____ 11. Family members shared interests with one another.
_____ 12. Rules changed often in our family.

Now add up the totals for the odd and then the even statements and place them below.

Totals: _____ Even-numbered statements

_____ Odd-numbered statements

Place the even-numbered total on the Adaptability scale and the odd-numbered total on the Attachment scale.

ADAPTABILITY SCALE

Chaotic					Adaptable				Rigid		
6	7	8	9	10	11	12	13	14	16	17	18

ATTACHMENT SCALE

Disengaged					Attached				Enmeshed		
6	7	8	9	10	11	12	13	14	16	17	18

Adaptability—chaotic and rigid families have poor problem solving capacities ingrained in their members, as well as having a hard time dealing with emotions.

- Rigid: Authoritarian, rules clear and non-negotiable.
- Chaotic: No leadership, unknown arbitrary rules, decisions made in crises neither planned nor well thought out.
- Adaptable: Clear but flexible leadership and healthy but adjustable discipline. Problems discussed and various members may input for a decision.

Attachment—disengaged and enmeshed, has difficulty building healthy marital relationships. Relationships are either too close, or too far. Personal and family boundary confusion is present.

- Enmeshed: No individuality desired or fostered, extreme sense of closeness. Independence looked upon as disloyalty. Boundaries nonexistent within the family, but members keep others outside the family.
- Disengaged: Value independence, and relationships outside the family. Little togetherness.
- Attached: Sense of individuality without a loss of connectedness. Do things together, but able to be active outside the family as well. Mutual respect that allows freedom of activity without hidden agendas that trigger guilt.

The closer each linear scale is to the middle, the healthier the family. There are usually combinations taken from each scale. Example: rigidly disengaged. Wherever you end up on the scales, do not be dismayed. The goal is information and bringing how your family is/was, to the Force (to the light).

3

LETTING GO OF CONTROL TO THE FORCE

God's Principles: Salvation and Letting Go

SALVATION

SALVATION IS THE act of being saved. When Jesus said, "I am the door. If anyone enters by Me, he will be saved..." (John 10:9), He was speaking immediately of being saved from the penalty of sin and ultimately from the power and presence of sin. The penalty of our sin is eternal separation from God, which He doesn't want anyone to choose. According to John 3:17, "God did not send His Son into the world to condemn the world, but that the world through Him might be saved." Jesus paid the price for your sins on the cross and it is only through Him that you will be saved. It's your choice.

In the Old Testament, only the chief priest was allowed into the Holy of Holies once a year to make atonement for the people before God. When Jesus died, the veil (curtain that was about 60 feet in height, 30 feet in width and four inches thick) that covered the opening to the Holy of Holies supernaturally ripped starting at the top, signifying that the way to God was open to all who believed in Jesus' shed blood for their sins. Jesus also said, in John 3:3—"Most assuredly, I say to you, unless one is born again, he cannot see the kingdom of God." It is when you accept Jesus' shed blood for your sins that He sends His Holy Spirit, God's holy Force, to live within you to guide and speak to you. In 2 Corinthians 6:16, God said, "...I will dwell in them and walk among them; And I will be their God, and they shall be My people." (NASB) When you accept the above, you become a child of the Most High God and God, in the person of the Holy Spirit, comes to dwell in you to lead and guide. He is a powerful Force and not to be taken lightly. He is not to be used by you but seeks rather to use you in loving God and others; even your enemies. The word, "HE" is used to describe the Holy Spirit (God's holy Force), as He is the third person of the trinity. The trinity is God, the Father, God, the Son (Jesus Christ), and God, the Holy Spirit. Each person of the trinity is God, but in different forms. Much like ice, rain, and steam are all water in different forms, God, the Father, reveals Himself to you by sending Jesus in human form, and then sends the Holy Spirit to dwell in you. To dwell in you, who sincerely believe and accept Jesus' death and resurrection as payment of your sins and who also submits to His lordship. In other words, God, in the form of the Holy Spirit (henceforth called God's holy Force), comes to dwell with and in you and in each of us who accepts Jesus' work on the cross!

FAITH

Faith is belief and trust in what God says. It is turning away from unbelief, "casting all your cares upon Him, for He cares for you" (1 Peter 5:7). Faith is not only an intellectual acceptance of the truth but also a positive recognition and conviction of the truth as stated by God's Word. Paul wrote in Romans 10:17, "Faith comes by hearing, and hearing by the Word of God."

The issue is our unbelief. Sometimes we, as believers, do not recognize nor believe that God is really interested in us or in every minute detail of our lives. We forget our privileged place before Him, as His sons and daughters, and so we struggle. We stop believing that God's holy Force is interested in directing us, guiding us, talking to us, and truly touching us, so we run. We are alone again. Well, why should we believe? No one else was there for us as we were growing up. Why should God be there?

Because He is, always was, and always will be the PERSONAL God that He is. What is your view of God? How limited is it? Do you dare to limit the Creator of the heavens and the earth? Yes, you likely do, as we all do. However, your belief and view of God and the limits that you place on Him affect your response to Him and His Word.

What is your worldview? Do you believe and LIVE the belief that God made the earth and all that is in it? That He has a plan for the world and for you as expressed in His Word? Do you live the belief that Jesus won victory on the cross over sin and death?

It is one thing to confess belief and another to live it. As you become aware of any unbelief you may have, confess it to God and to others and ask God to remove and heal that area in your life. That way, you can live your profession of faith in honesty before God. In other words, it's OK to have unbelief but it's not OK to stay there. So, don't be afraid of any unbelief but acknowledge it and bring it to the light so that God's holy Force can work in and with you, regarding your unbelief.

The journey you are on is one of learning to trust God and others with your very self. That is a sacred trust, considering that you and we are all "fearfully and wonderfully made" (Psalm 139:13). How precious are you, His creation! Do you recognize and truly or wholeheartedly believe this? Though people in your past and present have likely harmed you, thus creating the potential for a skewed view of God and others, God wants you to know that HE CREATED YOU, KNOWS YOU, AND IS WITH YOU, even if you do not FEEL His presence. "We walk by faith, not by sight," says God's Word (2 Corinthians 5:7). Know for sure that God is looking out for your best, wants to communicate His plan for and TO you, and is waiting for you to want to hear and then, to sit and listen to what He has to say for your life. Your personal healing and faith will abound as you begin to recognize how much God really loves you.

CONTROL

Control is trying to work things out on our own. It's a type of control that leads to bondage. It is a fallacy to believe that if you control things you will get what you want and will be happy. When you control others or yourself, you put a box around them and yourself. You place yourself in bondage to control. You are not free to be who God made you to be.

Controlling is an attempt to gain something for yourself or to protect yourself and there are two issues here:

- The other person is not allowed to freely choose to give you what you want. You might attempt to manipulate them and play games with them. Whatever you will obtain won't satisfy because deep down, you know what you received was not freely given, thus not worthwhile or true.
- Controlling protects yourself from your emotions and what you truly feel. You may not trust yourself to honor your opinions or emotions, so you put control around yourself as a protective measure. This lack of trust in Jesus Christ and in yourself is a faithless and ineffective way of dealing with the fear of the unknown.

Control and manipulation is the opposite of faith, which is opening up, letting go, and turning your life over to God, surrendering to His godly Force in the universe, the Holy Spirit. Submitting yourself to Jesus Christ means not trying to manipulate things to go your way.

Letting go of control does not mean you are a doormat and have no responsibility for your present or future. Quite the opposite. True acceptance of the responsibility for yourself and your actions happens. As you do this, you then begin to let go of all the shoulds, should nots, ought nots, have to, and need to, that you have been living by. How does this begin?

It begins by accepting responsibility for your behavior, which is difficult. It's so difficult you may live in denial, believing that you are good or that everything is fine. That only serves to bind you in discouragement, despair, and fear because you are not being truthful or honest. As you let go and hold out your hand in faith, you will move into the light where denial can be broken. You let go of your own control and the shutters begin to open. You begin to see your distorted perceptions of reality that have fostered destructive behaviors and begin admitting your responsibility for them. You begin to truly recognize that you are a sinner and even though you are, you begin to realize that you are loved and accepted, regardless of what you have done.

In letting go of control, you decide to stop fighting the reality of who you are, which is a waste of time and get to accept yourself as Jesus Christ accepts you; just as you are. This does not mean you will stay that way, but it is the place to start. With this acceptance and surrender, you let your walls down and unflinchingly realize how human and imperfect you are. You begin to live in the truth about yourself and being looking with understanding and compassion on yourself—something that's not easy to do! You become teachable and willing to listen to others. Communication begins to flourish and you can begin to feel connected. As this love and acceptance of yourself increases, you can in turn, understand and love others. After all, the second greatest commandment is to LOVE YOUR NEIGHBOR AS YOURSELF.

This chapter is asking you to make a commitment to lay down your own will and life to God the Father, God the Son, and God, the Holy Spirit. God is Lord, whether we accept this truth or not. There is acknowledgement of His Lordship and submission to it. It is decision time.

The first chapter covered the covenantal God who loves you, and in the second chapter, that you are not all powerful.... that there is one who is more holy and powerful than you are and He is a Person, Jesus Christ. Now you can take action on that knowledge by submitting yourself to His Lordship. If you have not yet asked Jesus to forgive your sins and come into your life but are sincere about asking Him in, pray the following out loud to be born again spiritually into God's kingdom:

Jesus, I am a sinner. I accept your sacrifice on the cross for my sins. I ask that You forgive me of my sins and come, dwell in my heart forever. I ask you to be my Lord and Savior. I know you died and rose again for me so that I may have eternal life (Romans 10:9-10). I recognize that by receiving Your forgiveness, that this does not give me liberty to go out and continue sinning or doing wrong. I want to learn of and follow Your ways. So Jesus, come into my life. I welcome the Holy Spirit and ask that He teach me Your ways.

Amen.

Congratulations! If you have asked Jesus to be your Lord and Savior and to come into your heart, you are now a child of God! Welcome to the family of God! You now have His Holy Spirit (God's holy Force) living within you to be your counselor, give you wisdom, direct your path, and more. A caution—God's force in you is not to serve you, but to guide you in serving others in love. Below are some scriptures to think about and memorize.

Matthew 16:24-25—"If anyone desires to come after Me, let him deny himself, and take up his cross, and follow Me. For anyone who wants to save his life will lose it, but anyone who loses his life for My sake will find it."
Matt 6:25-34—"Do not worry about your life, what you will eat or what you will drink…for tomorrow will worry about its own things. Sufficient for the day is its own trouble."

John 15:5—"I am the vine, you are the branches. He who abides in Me, and I in him, bears much fruit; for without Me, you can do nothing."

Ephesians 1:17—"May [God] give to you the spirit of wisdom and revelation in the knowledge of Him."

Describe turning your will over to Jesus:

_____

_____

How do you think Jesus sees you, your life, and your problems? What do you feel He is thinking about you?

_____

_____

_____

What doubts do you have that God can change you and your life for the better? _____

_____

_____

What fear do you have in trusting God with EVERY detail of your life? _____

_____

_____

What areas are you unwilling to turn over to God?

_____

_____

_____

How do you expect the Lord to help your path become straight?

_____

_____

How will giving your life over to God help to lessen the stress in your life?

_____

_____

What does God say about worry, in Matt 6:25-34? "Do not worry about your life, what you will eat or what you will drink…for tomorrow will worry about its own things. Sufficient for the day is its own trouble."

_____

_____

What are you willing to do to remove worry from your life? _____

_____

▲ ▲ ▲

LETTING GO

The Bible is a book about relationships and responsibilities and the following statements express our responsibility to people we have relationships with. As we seek to understand how this works, God will teach us.

To let go doesn't mean to stop caring; it means I cannot do certain things for others.

To let go is not to cut myself off; it's the realization that I cannot control others.

To let go is not always to shield, but to allow learning from natural consequences.

To let go is to admit powerlessness, which means the outcome is not in MY hands.

To let go is not to try to change or blame others; I can only change myself.

To let go is not to care for, but to care about.

To let go is not to judge, but to allow others to be human.

To let go is not to be in the middle arranging all the outcomes, but to allow others to affect their own outcomes.

To let go is not to deny, but to accept.

To let go is not to be overly protective, but to allow others to face reality.

To let go is not to nag, scold, or argue, but to search out my own shortcomings and correct them.

To let go is not to adjust everything to my desires, but to take each day as it comes and cherish the moment.

To let go is not to criticize and regulate others, but to try to become what God means ME to be.

To let go is not to regret the past, but to grow and live for the future.

To let go is to fear less, hang on, and trust in CHRIST more; freely giving the love He has given to me.

author unknown

Who or what do you need to let go of: a rebellious child, a sorrow, a lost loved one, or heartache you cannot change? Read this over, study it, pray over it, and you will find that letting go of your burden to God will release His peace to you.

In relationships, I see myself trying to manipulate in the following ways: _____

_____

In relationships, blaming often plays a big part in the communication process, which hinders intimacy. Instead of a win/win situation, there is usually an I won/you lost or you won/I lost scenario, which hurts intimacy.

My communications are usually: Me winning, You winning, or Us winning. (circle the one that applies)

I see myself blaming others most of the time for: _____

_____

_____

I blame myself for: _____

_____

God asks that you work with others where they are and love them unconditionally. That does not mean that you do not address issues in a relationship. Look at THE WAY IT IS MEANT TO BE in the appendix to answer the following questions.

What is stated about our purpose in living?

_____

_____

What is stated about loving others without controlling them?

_____

_____

What does losing myself to others mean?

_____

_____

I can best not lose myself to others by: _____

_____

Why must a relationship be established by choice and not guilt or manipulation?

_____

_____

⌁ ⌁ ⌁

4

TAKING STOCK WITH THE FORCE

God's Principles: Humility, Honesty, and Forgiveness

REVIEW "My PRAISE Song," found in the appendix.

"My Praise Song" talks about living and experiencing life freely. It talks about feeling the pain and sorrow in order to fully appreciate and experience joy! Living fully human, fully alive! Are you doing that? This chapter will support that type of living and set you on a course to live life fully.   Are you ready?

HUMILITY

Humility is an attitude of the mind, requiring honesty. It is acknowledging the truth about yourself and not thinking more or less of yourself than who you are. It is also looking out for others and not demanding that you be served or get your own way. Read Philippians 2:7. Jesus emptied Himself, which is our example to follow.

Humility is an attitude of serving. It is neither self-centered nor self-conscious. Self-consciousness is an area that many, if not all of us, need healing in. What would others think? How do I look? Am I accepted? Will others like me? The focus is on obtaining approval from others (man) rather than from God, who views believers as His wonderful creation in Christ. As you look to understand others and yourself from God's perspective, humility begins to bloom.

HONESTY

Honesty is reality and truth according to the Word of God and acknowledging what is really happening inside us. Honesty is hindered whenever we do not face the reality that is happening in our lives or how we really feel as fallible human beings. Denial at times serves to protect us (as a coping mechanism in a death situation), but most of the time it keeps us living a lie. Denial does not allow issues or emotions to be brought to the light where God's principles and healing touch can help us. It is like wearing a pair of rose-colored glasses, which enables us to walk around as though everything is rosy yet we aren't seeing reality. It is imperative that you seek to live honestly before God so that you can be set free. Ask for denial to be broken in your life and as you grow, God will make you as you were meant to be. God commands every believer to put away lying: "Let each one of you speak truth with his neighbor" (Ephesians 4:25). That requires all of us to be self-evaluators. Therefore, be honest with yourself about your sin and don't attempt to justify or rationalize any sinful behavior.

FORGIVENESS

Why forgiveness? Because our lives depend on it. Many times you might think that what another does is unforgivable—that the individual does not deserve to be forgiven. You likely would hold onto resentment and anger towards that person as a weapon against them. Are they aware of those feelings? Many times not. Do they care? Many times not. In reality, the weapon serves to destroy your relationship with God, your relationships with others, and with yourself. Negative feelings control you and you, who might think you are in control, are not. As tapes from the past play over and over again, your mental health erodes. God says that He alone is the avenger—He will repay (Romans 12:19). I remember thinking to myself as I was harboring ill will towards others, "I wouldn't want to be around someone who was always feeling like this, and here I am....always around myself!" The point is that I chose to no longer hold onto any negative feelings, as I didn't want to live with *myself* that way. It worked, and I now walk around in peace! We all have a relationship with ourselves and so, the question comes to mind; how do you want to live with yourself?

Stating the need for forgiveness does not mean that your hurt feelings are unjustified. What gets to happen is for each of us to look beyond the hurt and anger and allow ourselves to acknowledge/admit the *reason* for the pain. Our growth is enabled through experiencing, understanding, and speaking about what has happened to us. Doing this also breaks the power that the feelings have over us. There is a lie that states, "If you don't feel it, then it doesn't exist." Many feelings exist whether we want them to be present or not. When we don't acknowledge their presence, they can toss us to and fro, battering us to death. If you earnestly pray for self-awareness, God's holy Force will support you in your awareness of your feelings; "bringing every thought into captivity to the obedience of Christ" (2 Corinthians 10:5).

In forgiveness, it is important to look at the responsibility you might have played in allowing a situation to happen. Many people fail to take responsibility at this point and as such, are never truly free. Ask yourself, were my expectations too high? Were they unrealistic? When you set unrealistic expectations on others or yourself, you set up them and yourself for failure.

So why forgive? Because God demands it. In the Lord's Prayer, there is a statement of concurrence (something happening at the same time); "forgive us our debts as we (same time as) forgive our debtors." Jesus went on to explain, "If you do not forgive men their trespasses, neither will your Father forgive your trespasses" (Matthew 6:15). Forgiveness does not mean that what happened was OK or that you are to continue being a doormat and getting hurt. It means that you choose not to be controlled by a root of bitterness, anger, or resentment that kills you from the inside out. With forgiveness comes peace and serenity. If you choose not to incorporate this principle into your life, then you are also choosing to disobey God. The consequence is turmoil, lack of peace, and separation from Him.

For those who do not know how to forgive, it starts with trying to understand your own shortcomings and humanity. As you openly acknowledge your sinful nature, the walls you might have built to protect yourself can fall and you can then begin to look at others with more understanding and compassion. There is a reason for all behavior. Perhaps others were never taught what you were as they were growing up and yet, you might be expecting them to be the same or to know what you might think they should know. Society and each of us place expectations on others as well as ourselves that are not beneficial. Look at forgiveness as a vital part of fulfilling the second greatest commandment, "Love your neighbor as you love yourself" Matthew 22:39.

▲ ▲ ▲

My Self-Evaluation

Many times, individuals might come up to you and give you a compliment and yet you might turn the blessing away. It is sometimes hard to recognize the good qualities that are in each of us. For this exercise, look for good things in yourself and notice if good things are hard for you to identify. Then list the weaknesses that you have seen. To get you started, an example of strength is your willingness to learn and your commitment to going through this book! A weakness would be perhaps a lack of discipline in getting through one chapter in a week.

STRENGTHS   WEAKNESSES

_____   _____

_____   _____

_____   _____

_____   _____

_____   _____

From here, writing a self-evaluation is a logical step. The purpose of writing a self-evaluation is an open admission of what you have done wrong. It's being honest with yourself. It's in this admission that you can be freed from the guilt that plagues you. It is best to write down everything, as this helps to clarify your thoughts and facilitates discovery. There are questions to guide you and you can write whatever you want. In writing, you may be afraid of exposure, welcome it, or have elements of both operating in your life. This is to be expected but do not run and hide! No one will see this information unless you decide to share it with them. Remember, the Force is with you so you are not alone!

God can help you in writing your self-evaluation. Psalm 139:1-2 states, "O Lord, You have searched me and known me. You know my sitting down and my rising up." Seek God's assistance and He will freely give it since depending on Him is His will for you. He made and knows you!

Some have difficulty writing their self-evaluation for fear that God will not love them as He sees their faults. Rest assured that God knows already, for "there is no creature hidden from His sight, but all things are naked and open to the eyes of Him to whom we must give account" (Hebrews 4:13. Yet, He still loves us! Remember, God "has reconciled us to Himself through Jesus Christ" (2 Corinthians 5:18). Therefore, as you bring things to the light you are working together with Him and His principles. God is so happy when you do this evaluation, as He wants you to be free from anything weighing you down and bring all to the light! He is so happy you decided to not hide in the dark side!

In your self-evaluation, you may feel that you hurt others because they first hurt you. God says in Romans 12:17-19—"Repay no one evil for evil. Have regard for good things in the sight of all men. If it is possible, as much as depends on you, live peaceably with all men. Beloved, do not avenge yourself, but rather get rid of wrath; for it is written, Vengeance is Mine, I will repay, says the Lord."

What is God saying here about your response to others' actions or words against you?

_____

_____

What do you see that needs changing in your life to line up with what God is saying?

_____

_____

Denial has many faces including pretending, minimizing, blaming others, justifying behavior, and becoming angry to avoid an issue.

List examples of when you have denied reality:

_____

_____

Where do you see denial being most active in your life? _____

_____

_____

What anxieties do you have about past memories?

_____

_____

RESENTMENTS ARE DAMAGING AND CAUSE GREAT SPIRITUAL DISEASE

What is your major resentment, and how is it interfering with your life?

_____

_____

List situations where you become angry as a result of your resentments:

_____

_____

List your major fear and how it is interfering with your life:

_____

_____

What fear surfaces when you realize God knows all your faults?

_____

_____

What is your major strength, and how does it support you? _____

_____

_____

What is your major weakness, and how does it hurt you? _____

_____

_____

What is your resistance to completing this self-evaluation?

_____

_____

_____

I have decided to make the following goal/s (please see how to set goals in the appendix):

_____

_____

_____

▲ ▲ ▲

FIVE SAMPLE AREAS

The following are five different areas to support your self-evaluation, with the Holy Spirit's help. As you work through each area, think on it for a few days before you start writing. Let God's holy Force bring to remembrance what you can handle right now. Do not agonize in trying to remember everything the first time through. You can do this again years from now and you will be surprised at what God's holy Force will reveal that is new to you!

AREA ONE: FAMILY RELATIONSHIPS

Write down below how your family members treated you and you treated them. Were you close to them? What hindered your intimacy as a family?

_____

_____

_____

_____

_____

_____

_____

_____

_____

_____

_____

_____

_____

AREA TWO: SEXUAL CONSIDERATIONS
What were your first sexual experiences like? Were they before marriage? Multiple partners? Same–sex partners? What did your family tell you, or not tell you, about your sexuality? Were you sexually abused?

_____

_____

_____

_____

_____

_____

_____

_____

_____

_____

_____

_____

_____

_____

_____

_____

_____

_____

AREA THREE: AGES 0 – 12
Write down anything that stands out to you during these years. It could be good, such as playing soccer, or traumatic, such as being called names.

_____

_____

_____

_____

_____

_____

_____

_____

_____

_____

_____

_____

_____

_____

_____

_____

_____

AREA FOUR: AGES 13 – 18

Write down anything that stands out to you during these years. It could be about dating (or the lack thereof), how you were accepted (or not) by your peers, how you felt about school, your future plans in life, your relationship with your parents, and your teaching regarding God at this point in your life.

_____

_____

_____

_____

_____

_____

_____

_____

_____

_____

_____

_____

_____

_____

_____

_____

AREA FIVE: AGE 18 – PRESENT

Write about any area that stands out, such as relationships that did not work and why you think they did not work. Also write about lost dreams and emotional or sexual scars. Include any highlights.

_____

_____

_____

_____

_____

_____

_____

_____

_____

_____

You have a choice to do the following suggestion and doing so will cause a release to occur in you as the hidden parts you have written about are made known in the light. The suggestion is to share what you have written with someone of the same sex that you trust. It could be the opposite sex (spouse) if you know they will listen and not get upset about what you share. Please reference the next pages before you share with anyone. God will honor your courage in sharing your self-evaluation, so go with Him. His holy Force, is always with you!

Scripture to memorize this week: Psalm 51:1-4—"Have mercy on me, O God. Wash me thoroughly from my iniquity. My sin is always before me. Against You only, have I sinned."

▲ ▲ ▲

5

CONFESSION IN THE LIGHT OF THE FORCE

God's Principle: Confession

CONFESSION

IN CONFESSION, YOU verbally bring to the light what was previously in darkness. You don't want to be on the dark side, where John 3:20 says, "Everyone practicing evil hates the light and does not come to the light, lest his deeds should be exposed." Proverbs 28:13 says, "He who covers his sins will not prosper, but whoever confesses and forsakes them will have mercy." Mercy means having a pass or not receiving the judgement due us. Think of playing Monopoly and you get the free "Get Out Of Jail" card.   If you land on "Go to Jail", you get a pass. Proverbs says that if you confess and forsake (turn away from) your wrongdoings, you get a pass.   If you don't confess or forsake them, you don't get a pass and are held accountable for them and the consequences due.   I don't know about you, but I don't want any bad consequences! When I speak to God and tell Him my wrongdoings, He meets me, heals my heart, heals my emotions, and creates a right spirit within me.   I feel clean and clear of the fog and turmoil of my wrongs.   God knows my wrongs anyway but wants a relationship with me, and wants me to tell Him that I know I have done wrong and that I am sorry. That doesn't mean that I don't have to pay the consequences of my wrong doing, but it has been my life experience that as I confess my wrong, the consequences are not as terrible as they could have been.   God wants that with and for you, too! God wants all of us to confess not only to Him but also to each other, unless doing so would harm someone even more.   If confession would harm someone even more, sometimes writing a letter and then burning it clears emotions, our spirit, and the Force within us. Confession is one of God's principles for receiving mercy and living a victorious life. You cannot have a victorious life unless you incorporate this principle into your life. Ask God's holy Force and He will support you in doing this!

Scripture to memorize: Proverbs 28:13—"He who covers his sins will not prosper, but whoever confesses and forsakes them will have mercy."

SHARING YOUR SELF-EVALUATION

You might have already shared your self-evaluation with someone but if not, please keep several important factors in mind when deciding whom to share your self-evaluation with. It is advisable to choose someone of the same sex in order to be more open. Consider the following questions:

- Is the person trustworthy?
- Will they hold a confidence?
- How are their listening skills?
- Will they try to tell me what to do?
- Will they judge me as I share?
- Where do I want to hold this meeting?
- Will there be any distractions?
- What is the best time so we won't be tired?
- Will they be able to handle or accept what I tell them?

As you meet with your confidant, openly discuss confidentiality, what you wish to gain from the meeting, and the expectations you have for the meeting. When you finish, share with each other how you both experienced the sharing and what you have learned.

When you finish sharing, take a moment to fill out the following questions.

What feelings did you have as you were sharing your inventory?

_____

Other than being relieved, how did you feel on the inside after the process was over?

_____

How do you see God's principles healing you thus far?

_____

_____

What changes, if any, do you see in your behaviors, reactions, or attitudes during the time it took you to get to this chapter?

_____

_____

_____

What benefit did you receive from completing this chapter?

_____

_____

_____

▲ ▲ ▲

6

WILLINGNESS TO WORK WITH THE FORCE

God's Principles: Sanctification and Willingness

SANTIFICATION

SANCTIFICATION IS DEFINED as the process of the continuing work of God in the life of a believer, making him or her holy (more like Jesus). Sanctification can also be defined as being set apart, separate, or dedicated to a particular purpose or use.

As a child of God, sanctification will continue to occur throughout your lifetime, leading you into a life of increasing purity and goodness. There's good news in that God does not expect you to be perfect, although you may often expect that of others as well as yourself. He knew that you couldn't be perfect so He made provision for you through Jesus. Why, then, are you so hard on yourself and others? The grace, or unmerited favor, you have received from God allows you to stop trying to be perfect and be who you are. So don't pretend! Allow God's holy Force to change you from the inside out towards becoming freely loving and more like Jesus!

Sanctification, being a process, encourages you to be longsuffering towards yourself and others. You can allow the expectations of yourself and others to fall, knowing that we all are imperfect humans. What a refreshing thought and release this brings! It is much easier said than done but it is possible!

Even though God does not expect you to be perfect, that does not give you or anyone the liberty to do as they please, thinking it's OK to just ask for forgiveness. Rather, knowing that His ways are always best, you get to respond to His love and forgiveness towards you by seeking to do His will for your life.

WILLINGNESS

Willingness is an attitude of openness to change. It is saying, "Yes, I will' versus "No, I can't." There is no such truth as "I can't" when it comes to the will.   There's only, "I won't."

Fear and doubt get to be addressed with any unwillingness. At times, you may want to run but once you turn your thoughts away from the doubts and fears toward the issue at hand, your fear will lessen. Giving yourself permission to be open to change also lessens the fear and opens the door for the change to occur in thought and deed.

Willingness is a determination to do whatever it takes and to go the extra mile. It is a commitment to learning and understanding yourself, your world, and others. It is saying, "Yes, Lord, change me."

In this chapter, you are saying that you are willing for indwelling sin to be removed, not just lessened. God will respect your free will and move within you to free you, if you are entirely ready. This decision is saying that you are entirely ready to do business with God, and He with you. He is asking you, as He did the man whom He healed by the pool in John 5:6, "Do you want to be made well?" You may not want to be made well, but you can choose to be made well and the feelings will follow (obedience). If you do not choose to be made well, then it is your own responsibility for staying stuck where you are. God's holy Force is a gentleman and will not participate with you if He is not welcomed and asked. He won't force you to do anything. The choice is yours.

Do you want to be made well? _____

_____

What has God showed you that is to be removed, such as attitudes or heart motives? Refer to your self-evaluation in chapter 4.

_____

_____

What are you not entirely ready to have removed?

_____

_____

What is stopping your willingness in these areas?

_____

_____

What purpose has whatever you are holding onto, served in your life?

_____

What will you have to give up to be willing to be made well?

_____

_____

What feelings do you have when you think about being changed?

_____

_____

What behaviors have you tried in the past to change or fix within yourself and in your own power?

_____

_____

Whatever you are holding onto, how has that become part of your identity?

_____

_____

Oh, no! Don't tell me the way I identify myself may change or that I may have to take responsibility for myself!

In order to become entirely ready (a new attitude), you have a choice. You get to choose to be willing to change your pattern of reactions to people or situations in your life. Many times these patterns are so ingrained you may feel lost at the thought of them being absent or different. "Will anything take their place? Will I even exist or will I feel dead?" you may ask. Be not afraid! If you draw close to God, new thoughts, new attitudes, and new patterns following the mind of Christ will set you free! God's holy Force will gradually change you from the inside out as you take your wrong attitudes or actions to Him, confess them, and ask Him to forgive you.

Do you believe that God can uncover and remove those things that make you spiritually and emotionally sick?

_____

Why or why not?

_____

_____

What does Paul state in Philippians 2:13—"It is God who works in you both to will and to do for His good pleasure" about God's working in our lives?

_____

_____

God says in Isaiah 41:10—"Fear not, for I am with you. Be not dismayed, for I am your God. I will strengthen you, yes, I will help you. I will uphold you with my righteous right hand."

What does God say about any fear we may have about His working in our lives?

_____

_____

Scripture also affirms, "Now this is the confidence that we have in Him, that if we ask anything according to His will, He hears us. And if we know that He hears us, whatever we ask, we know that we have the petitions that we have asked of Him" (l John 5:14-15).   It is God's will that you depend on Him for everything, as He states in Philippians 4:6—"Do not be anxious about anything, but in every situation, by prayer and petition, with thanksgiving, present your request to God." If we are sincerely depending on Him for our healing, then it follows that He will do it, for setting us free from continual sin is part of His plan and according to His will.

Do you believe that God will do it?

_____

_____

Are you ready for Him to do it?

_____

Answer yes in the following space if you have asked God to do it:

_____

Ask God to change your will if your will does not line up with what He is telling you to do.   He loves you and wants you to love and come to Him with everything!

Scripture to memorize this week: Psalm 51:2—"Wash me from my iniquity, and cleanse me from my sin."

▲ ▲ ▲

MY MASKS

Masks are methods you may use to hide your feelings. In order to be whole as God intends you to be, become aware of your feelings so that they do not control you. Unawareness is a tool of Satan to keep you in bondage, but God has given you His Word "lest Satan should take advantage of us; for we are not ignorant of his devices" (2 Corinthians 2:11). If you are not aware of your feelings, how can you take them to God and talk to Him about them? How can you understand yourself (and others) if you are unaware of who you are and how you feel?

You may choose to use masks for many reasons including fear, insecurity, and shame. The focus will not be on the reasons, but on learning what masks you might be using and begin the process of removing them through truly loving yourself and by being loved by the most high God!

Masks vary. They can be ones of humor, busyness, happy go lucky, everything is always OK, cheerful, melancholy, being tough, and the like. Below, draw a picture of the mask/s you use most often to hide your feelings. Example—if you use cheerfulness as your mask, draw a smile. Another example—if you never show your feelings, your mask would be an emotionless, staring face.

Now, write down the feelings that are hidden behind your mask/s:

_____

_____

Before you go to bed, confess your masks to God and ask Him to remove them from your life.

▲ ▲ ▲

ABOUT ME

The following is an exercise to help you increase your awareness of your behavior. Once filled out, take someone trustworthy aside and share what you have written. Share your mask/s and the feelings that you hide when using them. It is self-disclosure that will facilitate the removal of the mask and the changing of your behavior. When you humble yourselves in honesty before God and others, the bondage can be broken. After you share with another, write down the feelings that you had during and after the sharing.

Some of my hopes are:

_____

I am most angry when:

_____

_____

I feel most sad when:

_____

_____

I run away from:

_____

Some people I care for are:

_____

I would describe myself as: (nouns and adjectives)

_____

_____

I feel most happy when:

_____

_____

Some feelings I have are:

_____

I am good at:

_____

My weaknesses are:

_____

_____

My strengths are:

_____

_____

After sharing, I feel:

_____

_____

▲ ▲ ▲

7

HUMILITY BEFORE THE FORCE

God's Principle: Repentance

A s you ask God for His will to be done in your life, He will begin to work. He knew you from the beginning, knows what will fulfill you, and is waiting for you to invite Him to work with you. What more could you want, for His will is perfect for you! Tell Him of any doubts and look for Him to work.

REPENTANCE

Repentance is a sincere, sorrowful acknowledgement of any wrongdoing, an acceptance of the responsibility for your erroneous ways, and a sincere, complete forsaking of those ways. The real issue is your heart attitude and whether you are sincerely serious about changing. Now you get to decide whether to give the reins to God to orchestrate your healing rather than trying to control or change yourself. You say, "Yes, Lord," and watch Him work. That does not mean He will heal you without any action on your part. Quite the contrary: This action requires repentance, taking to Him the error of your ways, asking Him to change you, and then looking to see what action He may require you to take to participate in your healing. The very act of repenting before Him brings release. When you sincerely repent, your attitudes, through the operation of God's Holy Force, begin to align themselves according to His attitudes. Other times, He may give you opportunities to practice the opposite of what you want Him to take away from you. For example, if you ask Him to take impatience away, He may begin to give you opportunities to practice patience.

As you come to Him in repentance, your sensitivity will grow in discerning the opportunities He is placing before you to practice the new skills He is working in you. It is up to you to walk through these opportunities. You will face a variety of temptations but know for sure that "no temptation has overtaken you except such as is common to man; but God is faithful, who will not allow you to be tempted beyond what you are able, but…will also make the way of escape, that you may be able to bear it" (1 Corinthians 10:13). *The way out is through*. As you do this, you will experience a strengthening and an understanding of His direction and operation in your life, which will enable you to open up to Him even more. Those around you had better watch out because soon you'll be flying instead of crawling!

Reasons to repent:

- God commands us to.
- Lack of honesty fosters ill health physically, mentally, spiritually, and relationally.

- All works will be shown in the end times.
- God knows anyway.
- Repentance is required for forgiveness, as it shows that you sincerely want to change.

How to repent:

- Sincerely ask God to change your heart attitude/s to align with His ways.
- Acknowledge what steps you can take to foster that change (e.g., treating others differently, being aware of self-serving motives and confessing them as needed).
- Accept God's forgiveness (not condemn yourself if you have sincerely repented).

You can tell you have truly repented if you are going in a different direction. An example is an army changing course when the general commands the change; it is noticeable immediately.

HUMILITY

According to J. Keith Miller in his book A Hunger for Healing (N.Y.: Harper Collins, 1991), humility is seeing yourself as you actually are; good and bad, strong and weak, and then acting authentically (honestly) on those truths. Without humility, you can't truly change as you are not fully open to being changed. And….humility is a choice. You can choose to lay your way down and ask God's Holy Force to show you His way.

Along with humility and honesty, congruence can happen. Congruence occurs when what is happening on the inside matches what is happening on the outside. Your mask is removed. Miller states, "As we let God remove that which we are not (what we are trying to be), and as we hear and try to be in fact what we potentially are, then we'll be more authentic. Living more in tune with the person God made us to be, we become free from the constant war that has gone on inside about what we should be and do in different areas of our lives" (pg. 120).

As you come to see that you are not God and cannot solve your problems alone, you can also begin to see that you cannot solve others problems for them. Each believer, according to Philippians 2:12, is responsible before God to work out their "own salvation with fear and trembling," which is a healthy desire to not offend God by disobeying Him. As you turn your problems over to God, you can also turn the problems of others over to Him to solve. Even though you do not carry the responsibility for another's problems, we all are commanded to "bear one another's burdens" (Galatians 6:2). In context, that means you are to stand with other believers, share each other's lives, sometimes help out with time or money, and pray for one another, but the responsibility for their lives stays with them, "for each one shall bear his own load" (Galatians 6:3). If you attempt to take on responsibilities that are not yours, that act of control and manipulation tempts others to remain as a child, which is a great disservice to them. The best thing you can do for others is point them to Jesus, allow them to do their own growing, and encourage and be there for them along the way.

Scripture to memorize this week: Matthew 7:7—"Ask, and it will be given to you; seek, and you will find; knock, and it will be opened to you." As you ask for God's will in your life, He will honor that and His Force will rise up within you and begin to show you things. Be careful here, as God's holy Force is not a genie, sent to do your bidding. You were created to do His bidding and to find and live out who He created you to be. You were created to do the works that He created for you to do even before you were born! You have a purpose! A HUGE purpose!

Why is humility so important in receiving God's help?

_____

_____

In what way have you seen humility open yourself up to God?

_____

_____

List some examples that show you are practicing humility:

_____

_____

What has God told you that has meant the most to you so far in your healing?

_____

_____

What one particular thing has God done for you so far through these chapters?

_____

_____

God says in Ezekiel 11:19-20—"I will give them one heart, and I will put a new spirit within them, and take the stony heart out of their flesh and give them a heart of flesh."

How is God using His holy Force to change you?

_____

_____

_____

With God's holy Force within you working to make you more like Jesus, you will be amazed that an increasing desire grows to be obedient to His will and way. As you follow Him, you will experience the blessings that are yours—only yours. Holiness is so much more than a matter of do's and don'ts; it is a heart that longs for obedience to God and increasingly is!

How have you seen your heart change thus far?

_____

_____

In what areas do you want obedience to occur?

_____

_____

My understanding of repentance is:

_____

_____

What fears do you have when you contemplate repentance?

_____

_____

_____

Letting go of things, even in repentance, entails a loss. Being human, you likely will or have grieved when you experienced a loss, which is not a comfortable experience. You may not want to feel your grief and may run from letting go of things in your life; even when you know you will benefit. With any loss, turn to God and ask Him to help you let go and participate with Him in getting rid of what He wants to get rid of, in your life.

(See the Grief Process in the appendix.)

What is your fear of feeling your pain?

_____

_____

What do you fear will happen if you let go of something that you have been holding onto?

_____

_____

_____

List the people, situations, and sins you are still holding onto when you know you shouldn't and the reason you are holding onto them.

	people/situations/wrong doings	reason
1.		
2.		
3.		
4.		
5.		
6.		
7.		
8.		
9.		
10.		
11.		
12.		
13.		
14.		
15.		
16.		
17.		

▲ ▲ ▲

8

True Forgiveness with the Support of The Force

God's Principles: Resentment and True Forgiveness

Forgiveness

If you hold bitterness towards others and condemn them, who do you think is paying for this? DO YOU WANT TO LIVE WITH YOURSELF with BITTERNESS AND YUCKY FEELINGS INSIDE? Do you want to walk through your life this way? Do you want to be like those you condemn? Unforgiveness is like keeping a garbage bag on your back filled with all the hurt you have received, which only serves to weigh you down and keep you in pain. Unforgiveness only hurts you. The other person/s involved in the situation likely don't remember what you did or what they did to you.   But you remember, because what they did hurt you.   Holding onto hurt only serves to keep you from having healthy and whole relationships.   God also says, "Forgive, and you will be forgiven."   This scripture tells you to forgive first, and you will then be forgiven.

You get to do what you can to repair the broken and bruised relationships of the past as you can't move forward to the present and future unless you do.   You get to address the relationships that have caused guilt, shame, pain, and resentment, as they continue to distance you from God, others, and yourself. If you do not release your negative pent-up emotions from all the guilt and pain in your life, they will skew a realistic viewing and evaluation of all your present relationships. Now this does not mean that you are to keep harmful relationships in your life. Addressing relationships means to evaluate the harm you have done to others, to yourself, and what others have done to you. It is taking responsibility for your actions, confessing the same, and asking for forgiveness. It is forgiving others and yourself. This is a preparatory step to moving out and loving others and yourself (the beginning of reconciliation). This chapter also asks if you are willing to make amends to ALL.

As you walk this path of life, God's holy Force can support you as you begin training yourself to catch yourself as you justify or explain away your behavior. If your behavior is wrong, why justify it? Just admit it and when you acknowledge it as such, distortion and denial of the truth fall away. When you admit wrong doing right away, you won't have to ask for forgiveness later and relationships work much better! When there are conflicts, acknowledging the wrong, your sorrow for the wrong, and your responsibility first and quickly will usually open the door to why the scenario went as it did. That is how looking with understanding begins between individuals and prevents more hurt from happening to or through you. Catching yourself early will stop many relationships from going sour. To support this process, we will discuss a tool to easily do this, in a later chapter.

Scripture to memorize: Luke 6:37—"Forgive, and you will be forgiven."

To help identify relationships that have hurt you, make a list of the people you get to forgive and the offense involved.

                   Person   Offense

1. _____   _____

2. _____   _____

3. _____   _____

4. _____   _____

5. _____   _____

6. _____   _____

7. _____   _____

8. _____   _____

Many times you may not realize how you are hurting others or how they are hurting you. Here are helpful guidelines for identifying harmful situations and knowing what to do.

- Someone is accusing you of doing something hurtful. Instead of being defensive, listen carefully and maybe take notes. Evaluate the criticism. Don't justify the behavior.
- Are you telling others what to do and giving your opinion even when it is not desired? That can be a form of controlling, even though as Christians we think we are being helpful and know what is right.
- Be sensitive to communication interplays. What stopped the flow? Did you say something that might have harmed the other and shut down the communication process? Stop right away and ask. It is better to clarify than to walk away not knowing what happened. If you walk away without the error's being addressed, the next time you meet the individual there may be residual reservations to entering a conversation since the previous conversation had no resolution or was uncomfortable.
- Are you blaming others or using the silent treatment? Blaming destroys others and you. No one prospers under the silent treatment, so let go of blame and open up the conversation. Begin talking!

As you move along these chapters, you likely have begun to see that the values that society promotes—status, control, excitement, and fun, are not the important things in life. Rather, as your masks diminish and God's holy Force awakens within you, perhaps you see that the important things in life are loving, intimate, and healthy relationships. Especially an open, intimate relationship with God, our Father. This, in turn, will give you more serenity and the ability to really enjoy living. This allows you to stop running, sink your roots down, and be yourself.

What harmful behaviors do you see yourself doing in relationships (e.g., gossiping, or being domineering, sarcastic, aggressive, or passive)?

_____

_____

Why do you think you operate this way?

_____

_____

What does God say is your responsibility toward others, in Romans 3:10—"Love does no harm to a neighbor?"

_____

_____

How can you become more sensitive to when harm is being done in a relationship?

_____

_____

Give an example where you noticed relational harm being done and you took steps right away to rectify the harm:

_____

_____

How would any unforgiveness on your part serve to block your progress and hurt your relationship with God? You can look up Matthew 6:14-15—"If you forgive men their trespasses, your heavenly Father will also forgive you. But if you do not forgive men their trespasses, neither will your Father forgive your trespasses."

_____

_____

God says, in Romans 12:19—"Do not avenge yourselves, but rather give place to wrath (put anger and vengeance away); for it is written, 'Vengeance is Mine; I will repay,' says the Lord."

What does God say about His responsibility towards those who harm/hurt you?

_____

_____

What feelings come up in you at the command that it is not your place to get even with others—that it is God's place?

_____

_____

Do you believe that others will get their due?

_____

What reluctance do you have to let Him give others their due?

_____

_____

Many times you will not see others get their due. You may be out of their lives when their due comes to them but you can rest assured that ANYONE who does not commit their lives to God's way will pay; either in this life or the life to come. Making amends means to attempt to heal the relationship through communication or actions, such as restitution (giving back more than what was stolen, i.e., making things better than they were).

How will letting go of unforgiveness and making amends set you free? _____

_____

_____

_____

What do you hope to gain by making amends? _____

_____

_____

_____

What do you fear most in making amends? _____

_____

_____

_____

The following prayer will support you as you decide to release others and/or yourself from the slavery of pent up negative shame, blame, guilt, and expectations, to name a few. Say the prayer out loud and fill in the blanks with who you are releasing from the jail house of your resentment.

A PRAYER FOR RELEASE FROM RESENTMENT
By Peter Marshall, Congressional Chaplin

Lord Jesus, You know me altogether. You know that I have steadily refused to forgive this one who has wronged me, yet have had the audacity often to seek Your forgiveness for my own wrongdoing.

The acids of bitterness and a vengeful spirit have threatened to eat away my peace. Yet I have stubbornly rationalized every unlovely motive. I have said, "I am clearly in the right. It is only human to dislike a few people. This one deserves no forgiveness." How well I know that neither have I ever deserved the forgiveness, which You have always freely granted me.

So, Lord Jesus, I ask You now for the grace to forgive this hurt. Even now, I am divided about it, only partially willing to release it. But you can manage even my reluctance, my loitering feet. Take now my divided will and make it of one piece, wholly Your will.

And Lord, I give to You this emotion of resentment, which clings as if glued to my heart. Wrest it from me. Cleanse every petty thought. Make me sweet again. I dare to ask that You will not only forgive me to the extent that I have forgiven _____, but that You will bless _____ to the degree that You have blessed me. For these great mercies I thank You, in Your name, who gave me the supreme example in forgiving even those who slew You. Amen.

Peter Marshall—Chaplain of the U.S. Senate from 1947-1949. cited in The Prayers of Peter Marshall by Catherine Marshall (N.Y. : Inspirational Press ed., 1996), p. 324. Updated Thee and Thy usage.

⋏ ⋏ ⋏

9

RECONCILE WITH THE SUPPORT OF THE FORCE

God's Principle: Reconciliation

RECONCILIATION

IN ONE SENSE, God's whole message centers around this principle. If you do not incorporate this principle in your life, God's peace will not be yours. Reconciliation denotes a change; usually from enmity to friendship. God opened the door to Himself by sending His Son, Jesus, to die for you so that you may enter a covenant relationship with Him. In other words, God sent Jesus to reconcile you, through Jesus' death and resurrection, with Himself and through Jesus there is no barrier to unity and peace with our Maker, God.

Reconciliation with others also denotes leaving NO impediment to unity and peace. Hence, no bitterness, evil thoughts, unforgiveness, or anything hindering peace is to remain between individuals. Mutual concession may be necessary for that to take place. You, if a child of the most High God, are called to be a peacemaker and treat others as you would want to be treated. Being a peacemaker requires responsibility on your part to try to repair broken or wounded relationships, even if you are not the one who did the wrong.

Cultivating a sensitivity of your relationship with God and others empowers you to be aware when friction is present in a relationship. An ounce of preventive maintenance is much better than a pound of cure, so address this friction right away so it does not fester and get worse.

Reconciliation takes place through confession, understanding, and forgiveness. With anything we do wrong, take your actions, emotions, motives, and thoughts to God and ask Him for forgiveness first and foremost. Be direct, honest, and brief, stating what has been done wrong to God and then to the other individual. Look to reconcile your relationship with God first, and your mind, spirit, and heart will be clearer as you attempt to be a peacemaker with others. Take responsibility for your behavior and the wrong attitude or motives that prompted it, expressing remorse. Training yourself to be a peacemaker and confessing and repenting of the heart attitudes that are keeping you from acting in God's ways are key to having harmonious relationships with God and others.

In approaching someone to make amends or reconcile with them, do know that there is risk with taking this action. You won't know whether you will be rejected or accepted for your efforts, especially when you try to make amends with your enemies. Still, you are called to make amends to all.

In attempting reconciliation, it is best to meet face to face whenever possible. Much is stated in non-verbal communication and you can better perceive whether amends are happening or not. If the person you want to make amends with has passed away, some individuals have found it helpful to write a letter telling the person what you would have said in person. It is in the confession of the spoken, written, or signed word that healing happens.

What are you to do if a person refuses to participate in the reconciliation process? For reconciliation to occur between two people, yes, it does take two. If another does not accept your attempt to reconcile the relationship, the next step would be to confess your part in the disparity of the relationship to God and accept His pardon. You may also feel it is necessary to confess your part to a close friend but first examine your motives. Do you want to gossip about so and so who does not want to reconcile the relationship or do you sincerely want to confess a wrong you did? Do you feel genuine sorrow and concern for the damaged relationship? Once you have done the above, you are free from your part in the reconciliatory process. The other person is guilty before God for not being willing to make peace. Then, just wait patiently, hoping and looking always for a change towards reconciliation. You do not get to keep going to the other person to try to fix the relationship only to get rebuffed time and time again, unless God's holy Force is prompting you to do so.

Apologies differ from reconciliation. You can apologize for doing something wrong, but unless your behavior changes (recall Chapter 7—repentance), reconciliation cannot happen and this sorrow is not heartfelt. Many individuals say they are sorry but are only sorry because they got caught. They are not sorry for the wrong that they did and don't plan on acting differently in the future. That is not true repentance and thus, reconciliation is not true from that person. Just evaluate yourself to ensure that you are not that person!

The biggest obstacle to making amends is pride. You may not want others to think less of you or differently towards you, so you hesitate. Actually, most of the time, the opposite happens. By your actions, people know you care about them, about yourself, and they respect you and appreciate your efforts. Pride binds but humility frees. Which do you choose?

Scripture to memorize: Matthew 5:9—"Blessed are the peacemakers, for they shall be called sons of God."

How has seeking revenge hurt you in the past?

_____

_____

_____

Feelings surface when we risk being honest with others about our feelings and faults. List those that come up for you:

_____

_____

_____

Give an example where you apologized but as it was not heartfelt sorrow, reconciliation didn't happen:

_____

_____

What feelings do you have when you contemplate trying to reconcile to your enemies?

_____

_____

_____

List an example and the result of a reconciliation that you have had with one of your enemies:

_____

_____

List an example and the result of a reconciliation that you participated in the past two weeks:

_____

_____

What were your feelings after you shared?

_____

_____

Sometimes situations will not require going to an individual for reconciliation to occur. You will know if this is the case and you can go directly to God, ask for forgiveness, and move on. You don't want to avoid your responsibility, so a close evaluation gets to occur in the decision about whether or not you are to go to that person. Perhaps more harm than good may occur? Wisdom is needed and seeking council may be in order.

Is there anything on your list of amends that may cause more harm than good?

_____

If so, which one and why?

_____

_____

When seeking reconciliation, it is necessary to pray for sensitivity in timing. In one situation, you may be able to make amends right away. In another, waiting for the right timing is best. Example: If your emotions are still too close to the surface, you may not be able to make a clean amend. A clean amend or reconciliation means that the attempt at reconciliation is not tainted AT ALL by anything other than wanting the relationship repaired. Evaluating, confessing, and repenting of your motives, your heart attitudes, and your emotions before you act is imperative on your part to make a clean reconciliation attempt to repair any relationship.

▲ ▲ ▲

10

HONESTY TO YOURSELF AND TO THE FORCE

God's Principles: Honesty and God's Spiritual Armor

HONESTY

As you have come through the previous 9 chapters, you have seen how God desires for you to walk. These last 3 chapters show how to maintain this walk so that you do not go back to old ways. Thus far you may have come from, "I am a wretched human being" to "I am a child of the Living God! I am special, molded for His unique plan for me! I have purpose! I am living in the present, not the past!" Romans 6:8 says, "Now if we died with Christ, we believe that we shall also live with Him." That is true not only for the future but also for now. "Likewise…reckon yourselves to be dead indeed to sin, but alive to God in Christ Jesus our Lord. Therefore do not let sin reign in your mortal body, that you should obey it in its lusts…for sin shall not have dominion over you…" (Romans 6:12-14). The command is clear and we get to choose to believe it and obey.

Chapter 10 incorporates using ALL the previous principles of God stated in the previous chapters. Chapters 1-3 are designed to help you release your emotions and accept the freedom from guilt and sin's power over you. Jesus gives this to you if you accepted (for you) that He died on the cross and rose again that third day to pay the penalty of your sins—past, present, and future! The first three chapters puts you in the right place to take an accurate personal self-evaluation in Chapter 4. Next are confession and reconciliation, as well as an attitude of readiness to have what you see in yourself removed or refined. Let's move on to other helpful self-evaluation tools to support being honest quickly.

SPIRITUAL EVALUATION

J. Keith Miller, in A Hunger For Healing, says that the three most common types of spiritual evaluations are the:

- On-the-spot check.
- Daily examination.
- Periodic examination.

The spot check is immediate, which requires a conscious attitude of hearing the Holy Spirit, God's holy Force, as He checks you on something. The daily inventory is best started in the morning by asking God to show you during the day (on-the-spot checks) your erroneous ways and then reviewing them with Him in the evening, looking towards change. The point is not becoming obsessed with monitoring yourself, but depending on God and His holy Force to show you. God is in control over your healing and your sanctification process, "for it is God who works in you both to will and to do for His good pleasure" (Philippians 2:13). How can it not work, if you do it the way it was set up and meant to be!

Chapter 10 speaks of living attentively but to not be obsessive. It asks you to do preventive maintenance and diligence to do what you have learned thus far. But, it is to be done only if you want to. You don't HAVE to do this. If you purpose to incorporate doing this in your life, you will be following God's way and He will bless you and His holy Force will begin to talk to and lead you. You do a brief daily examination of your strengths, weaknesses, motives, and behaviors and lay them all before God. It is keeping short accounts with Father God, so that the freedom you have experienced may continue. Cultivating the godly habit of conversing with God throughout the day and taking to Him all the concerns and cares that you have will keep you in tune with Him. Your antennae will be up. In taking all your cares to Him, imagine tossing a basketball into a closed net and the basketball stays there, right? With God, toss Him your care, He catches it and then keeps it! You leave it there in His hands (the closed net). Throughout your day, toss your concerns, worry, frustrations, and triumphs into His hands (the closed net) and watch the results!

An important element in your daily examination is not being a harsh judge of yourself. Let yourself off the hook! God's holy Force will show you what you are to know about where your thoughts and emotions are coming from (ex., motives, hurts) IF you sincerely ask Him to. God says, in John 16:13, "When He, the Spirit of truth has come, He will guide you into all truth...and He will tell you things to come." So, you are able to depend upon God's holy Force for discernment, as you will be bombarded by your flesh, the world, Satan (the father of lies—John 8:44), and his fellow demon liars. Satan and his forces seek to derail you, so be aware and don't let that happen! You won't be derailed if you stay honest with God and yourself and incorporate God's principles of honesty, confession, repentance, and reconciliation into your life.

Another helpful tool is writing in a journal. Writing can be a helpful way of keeping a daily inventory. It can be done as often and in any way you desire. You can begin a journal entry as a letter to God such as, Dear Lord, or however you want. You can write what is happening with you, what you feel God has been showing you, where you think He is leading you, and thank Him for being there with you. I have been doing that for many years and in looking at my old journals, I feel pleased and thankful in seeing the healing God has wrought in me and the growth that has taken place thus far. So far have I come, yet so far do I have to go! I encourage you to make use of the written word to help clarify thoughts and emotions racing around within you by writing in a journal. The matchless benefit will be a clear mind and eventually, clear direction!

The periodic examination can be done monthly or yearly. Take time for yourself to reflect on your growth. Read your journals and identify what is going on. You will know if you are on the right road or not and whether you get to repair a relationship that may have become tainted.

Scripture to memorize: John 16:13—"When He, the Spirit of truth, has come, He will guide you into all truth...and He will tell you things to come."

SPIRITUAL WARFARE

All warfare, in a sense, is from Satan because of the fall of mankind but it can be divided into direct and indirect warfare. Direct warfare is with Satan and his demons, whereas indirect warfare comes from within your flesh and through our society (the world with its lusts, power, and lies). If Satan can get through to you through the indirect method, then he can leave you alone to affect your own destruction. The world will pull at your flesh and be ever before you, bombarding most of your senses every day. That is why you get to know how to defend yourself spiritually.

FIGHTING THE FLESH

Romans 6 call you to not let sin reign in your mortal bodies, for until we all see Jesus, we still live in fallen human flesh that resists the redeemed spirit within. In Romans 7, Paul gives a personal illustration: "I know that in me I delight in the law of God according to the inward man.... With the mind I myself serve the law of God, but with the flesh, the law of sin" (vv.18-25). All Christians, from the mature Apostle Paul to the newest believer, have experienced the temptation cycle described in James 1:14-15. This starts with a desire, which you can choose to dwell on but if you do, your emotions will become stirred up. With the emotions stirred up, your desire increases. If you continue to nurse that desire, you will get to the point of no return and act on your desire, resulting in sin and its terrible consequences.

How do you handle your flesh? You first get to evaluate what is going on. Ask, "Am I tired and feeling a certain way due to lack of sleep or food? Are my closest relationships on open terms? Am I anxious about something? Is it time for my monthly cycle, if a female? Am I having a miscommunication problem with my friend?" If you cannot identify the reason for difficult emotions, thoughts, or feelings, do not despair! God commands us to cast away, or cast "down arguments and every high thing that exalts itself against the knowledge of God, bringing every thought into captivity to the obedience of Christ" (2 Corinthians 10:5). What this means, is to throw away any thoughts that show up in your mind, that are lies. Picture having the Word of God written on the backboard of your mind. When the troublesome thought comes, scan the backboard to determine whether that thought conforms to God's Word and if not, it's likely a lie and immediately toss it out of your mind. Using anger as an example, the Lord says in Ephesians 4:26-27 to "'be angry, and do not sin': do not let the sun go down on your wrath, nor give place to the devil." What this means, is you are giving place to the devil if you don't communicate or repair a relationship that is sour, and the anger is continuing to fester. As you hold onto anger, bitterness builds itself a root in you, which becomes Satan's playground to beat you down with. Again, allowing a root of bitterness to be planted and grow by not addressing issues, is giving place to the devil. It is laying a foundation with the enemy's tool of anger and bitterness, not God's way of honesty, confession, repentance, and reconciliation. This is why it is important to deal immediately with anger and other potentially negative emotions by speaking honestly yet gently with friends, to God, and to your family. Then, you get to let go of the emotions as talked about in chapter 3. Again, in Ephesians 4:26-27, God says to be angry but not to react with sinning behavior when we feel our anger. God gave us anger as it tells us that something is not right. Maybe someone is hurting us or hurting someone that we care about. Anger is a valuable emotion and learning from it will tell you much about yourself and what is going on around you.

FIGHTING THE WORLD

With the world, you must be careful in what you subject your eyes, mind, and heart to. Satan has perverted God's creation and principles so much that you must be careful of the magazines, books, movies, television shows, soap operas (they teach something other than God's beautifully ordained way of relating), MTV, pornography, and anything else that gives out lies and perversions of God's ways. There is no way you can prevent all from getting in, but you can control the amount you subject yourself to. You get to learn to detect the lies and unreality, as Satan's perversions are there. The best way to protect yourself is to know God and His ways by being a diligent student of His Word. An example of this is how a new bank teller is trained. In order to be able to feel the fake money, the bank teller handles the real money over and over and over until the teller can tell the difference between the fake and real bills. The bank teller doesn't study the fake money, but the real. This example speaks to studying God's true way and when you do, you will know the fake, perverted truth (lie) when it comes around.

FIGHTING THE DEVIL

Regarding Satan and his demons, Ephesians 6 explains that spiritual warfare is not ultimately against flesh and blood, but against principalities, against powers, against the rulers of the darkness of this age, against spiritual hosts of wickedness in the heavenly places (v.12). Here is God's provision for us: "Take up the whole armor of God, that you may be able to withstand in the evil day [a promise]… having girded your waist with truth, having put on the breastplate of righteousness, and having shod your feet with above all, the gospel of peace; taking the shield of faith with which you will be able to quench all the fiery darts of the wicked one. And take the helmet of salvation, and the sword of the Spirit, which is the Word of God; praying always with all prayer and supplication in the Spirit, being watchful to this end with all perseverance and supplication for all the saints" (vv. 13-18). You get to pray for yourself, each other, and put on the armor of God to fight the enemy who seeks to destroy you and your loved ones. Waking up each morning and intentionally speaking God's armor over yourself is very powerful in walking God's way and preparing yourself for the daily battle between the dark side (evil way) and God's way (holy, righteous, and good).

KINGS, PRIESTS AND SAINTS

Revelation 1:6 and 5:10 state, that God has "made us kings and priests." That means you are clothed in royal dignity, called to royal dominion. First Peter 2:5 declares, "You…are being built up [as]..a holy priesthood, to offer up spiritual sacrifices." You are in a priestly fraternity and priests are mediators, who bring others to God. A king is one who rules with authority and power. So are you wallowing in defeat? Rise up and fight, stepping out as the priest and king that you are (that includes women)!

Is there anything hindering you from accepting what God says you are--a priest and a king? Are you feeling unworthy? None of us are worthy, but God saw fit to send Jesus, as your savior and mediator. He then calls you and us all sons and daughters, priests and kings, because we are His. Not by anything we do, but because He says so. So, accept WHO you are because of WHO made you to be a priest and king!

Revelation 5:8 speaks of "the prayers of the saints." Anyone who has accepted Jesus' death and resurrection for their sins are also called saints! The Greek word, hagios, translated "saints", means to be set apart, to share in God's purity, and to be blameless, sacred, and pure. Christians are holy through the atoning work of Jesus. God sees us without spot or blemish through what Jesus did on the cross for us. He sees us flawless. As a Christian, do you see yourself as God sees you? If not, you will experience defeat. If so, you will experience victory!

Write down any other hindrances you feel in accepting the fact that as a child of God you are a priest, saint, and a king:

_____

_____

_____

Now, take these hindrances to God and ask Him to remove them, confess your unbelief, and choose to believe. Choosing to believe and speak what God says is key in keeping the victory in Christ that you have as His child. Does that mean that you will do things right all the time? Of course not, but the key is to confess it immediately and decide to turn from it (repentance).

Describe a situation where you were recently wrong and admitted it immediately:

_____

_____

What were your feelings before and after?

_____

_____

_____

Cite an example that shows you are learning new ways of interacting with others:

_____

_____

What does God say about what you are to do when others wrong you? Are you to confront them? Jesus said, "If your brother sins against you, go and tell him his fault between you and him alone. If he hears you, you have gained your brother" (Matthew 18:15). It does not say to go to Sally or Joe and gossip, but to the brother who wronged you. Going to the person directly involved is God's way of solving problems in the church with other saints (use wisdom and restraint in confronting non-Christians). You may hesitate going to the person because of fear but giving into fear only perpetuates the division in the relationship and God's way is harmony and unity. It is human nature usually to continue the way we are, unless someone else (ex., our boss) holds us accountable. Image a society where each individual holds themselves accountable! That would be heaven! So, God's way is to hold ourselves accountable. Therefore, holding yourself and others accountable to the way God has outlined for us to act in the scriptures fosters everyone's spiritual growth. You are loving people and love is actually shown to others when you care enough to confront (see Communication and Confrontation in the appendix). They may rebel and run, but that is their responsibility before God. Just make sure you are being responsible before Him to do your part.

Describe an example where you confronted your brother:

_____

_____

_____

What did you learn from this?

_____

_____

Describe an example where you did not confront but should have:

_____

_____

What feelings were not resolved?

_____

_____

What effect did that have on you?

_____

_____

Describe how you felt when writing down feelings or experiences on paper:

_____

_____

How much time do you spend evaluating and reflecting on your life?

_____

How much silence do you allow in your life?

In Joyce Huggett's book, The Joy of Listening to God, there is an example of a jar filled with water and sand. When the jar is shaken, the water is cloudy. As the jar rests, the sand settles to the bottom, and the water becomes clear. It is the same with our lives. Sometimes, our life's pace clouds our perceptions and listening skills. As we allow rest and silence, we can hear God speak and work within us, resulting in clear perceptions.

FASTING

Another way to listen to God is fasting. The following work,
written by Pastor Bill Robison, is adapted and used by permission.

What is the first thought that comes to your mind when you think of fasting? Do you picture some Buddhist monk or Hindu devotee? Perhaps the idea of fasting in a high tech world seems rather archaic. There might be some super-spiritual types who don't work who have time for this sort of thing, but how about a busy 40 + hour-a-week type?

Fasting is probably the most misunderstood and least practiced blessing that God has given to us so that we might draw closer to Him. Perhaps one reason is that it is practiced in all religions. Another reason is that in an age of fat phobia, fasting for physical rather than spiritual reasons is rather commonplace! Did you know that fasting is biblical and has always been part of the practice of God's church throughout history?

During the time of Jesus, fasting was a common practice among the Jewish people. John the Baptist and Jesus Himself practiced fasting when seeking the will of God. Even though it became a legalistic practice when used by the Pharisees, these scriptures reveal the biblical basis for fasting: Leviticus 23:27-28, Isaiah 58:1-7, Daniel 10:1-12, Nehemiah 1:4-11, and Esther 4:13-17. Fasting was always a part of the nation of Israel's life. We know that Moses, David, and Elijah fasted.

The early church practiced voluntary fasting rather than the mandatory form found in the Jewish tradition. By the second century, there were two days of voluntary fasting a week: Wednesday and Friday.

As the church became more institutionalized, fasting became more legalized and was misconstrued to be a form of penance useful in winning God's favor. After the time of martyrdom ceased, monks became the new heroes. The big thing was who could fast the longest. Unfortunately, it became more of a pseudo-spiritual ego trip rather than what God had intended it to be.

When the Protestant Reformation came about, many churches who wanted to break all ties with Catholicism had little use for fasting. In a very reactionary way, they threw out the baby with the bath water! Five hundred years have passed and fasting is still only minimally emphasized. How many sermons have you heard about it?

WHAT IS FASTING?

Here is a simple definition: Fasting is abstaining from food, drink, or both to draw closer to God. In an age with so many things that draw our attention, food and drink are primary things which do just that. We might say that fasting is the voluntary denial of an otherwise normal function for the sake of intense spiritual activity. Fasting is a useful tool for seeking a deeper level of communion with God in prayer and meditation, to receive guidance in decision making, and experience intimate fellowship with Him. An important issue to understand is that fasting is not done to appease or manipulate God.

PROBLEMS WITH FASTING

There are four basic problems with fasting today. First, fasting has a bad reputation. Second, most people are generally uninformed about it. Third, we have many misconceptions about our body's need for food. Finally, we have some misconceptions about the act of fasting itself.

Jesus Christ clearly taught on fasting, and fasted Himself. In Luke 4:1-13, we see that He fasted for 40 days without food. It does not say He went without liquids.

Matthew 6:16-18 instructs, "When you fast, do not be like the hypocrites, with a sad countenance. For they disfigure their faces that they may appear to men to be fasting. Assuredly, I say to you, they have their reward. But you, when you fast, anoint your head and wash your face, so that you do not appear to men to be fasting, but to your Father who is in the secret place; and your Father who sees in secret will reward you openly." Notice that Jesus did not attack the act of fasting or the frequency of it. As a matter of fact, Jesus assumed His disciples would fast. Fasting should be part of the life of a Christian. What Jesus did attack is fasting to impress people with one's supposed spirituality. As usual, Christ gets to the heart of the matter: He's concerned with WHY we fast, not just that we do it.

BASIC MODELS

There are three basic models of fasting in Scripture. We see a partial fast in Daniel 10:3. In this type of fast, a person goes without certain kinds of food or drink for a set time. Wisdom should be used when on a liquid fast rather than on a food fast because God designed the human body to require liquids much more often than food. The type of fast we see in Acts 9:9 and in numerous Old Testament scriptures is the complete fast or abstinence from food and drink for a period of time. Finally, we see the corporate fast, in which the whole nation was called to participate in Leviticus 23:27 and Joel 2:15.

There may be other types of fasts to help you focus on meeting with God. What distracts you or preoccupies you? For some, perhaps a fast from television, radio, movies, videos, or music would be appropriate. How about a fast from sports or a couch potato fast? Maybe start a fast by refraining from talking on the phone or just from talking? Find out personally how silence teaches one to listen well and speak more wisely.

HOW LONG SHOULD ONE FAST?

Remember the purpose in fasting. The issue is not how long the fast is, but whether you are meeting God. I have fasted a long time and not met God; I have fasted for only a short time and experienced wonderful times with Him. Some people fast from 6 p.m. until 6 p.m. the following day. Others go for 36 hours or only for a meal or two. I encourage you to start out easy if you have never fasted before. It is important to fast when you know you have the time or can make the time. I do not recommend fasting while you are at work or are engaged in strenuous physical activity. If you do fast during those times, you may find yourself getting very fatigued and not being able to accomplish anything positive. If you have any medical concerns, speak to your doctor before deciding upon the type and length of a fast. Be reasonable and realistic. Examine your heart: God is not out to have you break the Guinness World Record for super-spirituality!

When you fast, you will become aware of the things that control you. Your stomach is programmed to have food put into it even when you do not need it and your mind has the habit of reminding you when you have missed a meal. Don't worry: you can miss a meal and not die of starvation. If you do eat something, don't condemn yourself. God doesn't. You can't prove anything to Him anyway. He loves you, wants to be with you, and talk to you when you can give Him your undivided attention.

MY THOUGHTS

11

SILENCE AND SUBMISSION TO THE FORCE

CHAPTER 11 IS a continuation of all the previous steps combined. It is an earnest seeking for God in humble dependence. You can find Him in his Word and His creation, but what of when He speaks in "a still small voice" (1Kings 19:12)?

SILENCE

When you listen in silence, He speaks. He wants you to listen, but you are likely often running hither and thither. The more familiar you are with His voice the more often you will hear it, even in the midst of chaos. God says—"Be still, and know that I am God" (Psalm 46:10). Meeting frequently with the great "I am" is life changing. As you commune with the biggest lover of the universe, His love will flow through you in abundance! How joyful your heart will be as despair flees in His presence! How much bigger your worldview will be as you meet and spend time with Him.

Find a comfortable, consistent, and convenient place and time to meet with Him without distractions. That is one of the most practical ways to fulfill the first part of the Golden Rule commandment, which is loving God with all your heart, soul, mind, and strength. Spend time with Him!

Your intellect can get in the way of hearing God and seeing His work in your life. The intellect is very important and necessary for understanding and applying God's Word to your life but if carried too far, analysis paralysis can harden your heart and emotions to God's touch. Going one step further, overanalyzing can keep you out of touch with your own emotions. How can you give yourself to your Maker if you do not know who and whose you are? How can you experience your Maker if you are not even open to experiencing yourself? This state is often referred to as "frozen" or "cut off at the neck," which means that the heart is not felt. It is silent. The heart, emotions, and the mind are not working together. Only the mind is working, making decisions alone. How can you love the Lord your God with all your heart, mind, soul, and strength if you are not aware of each area within yourself?

How does analysis paralysis happen? Perhaps you were taught that emotions were not OK, so the ice began to build. Perhaps you made wrong choices and got hurt based on emotions, and consequently decided not to listen to them at all. There are many possibilities, but your purpose here is not to delve into why but to learn to open yourself fully to God and hear His voice in silence.

Chapter 11 is another tool by which you will sustain the progress made in chapters 1-10. Chapter 11 speaks to improving your conscious contact with the Trinity (God the Father, God, the Son, and God, the Holy Spirit). That requires some discipline on your part. To know a friend, you spend time with him or her, right? The same applies to God. To know Him, you get to spend time with Him. Jesus knew that God knows best, so He spent time praying to God to know His will. The best example He gave us was when He prayed, "Not My will, but Your will be done" (Luke 22:42). Also, our Lord taught us to pray, saying, "Your will be done on earth as it is in heaven" (Matthew 6:10). To be able to pray like that sincerely, your heart belief would be that God is interested in all that you do and all that happens to you. You believe that He has your best interest at heart though you may not understand fully. Do you believe? It's a choice to accept the truth that He loves you and is interested in you.   Making time for daily prayer and meditation will keep your growth moving forward by keeping you in close contact with God.

THE HOLY SPIRIT, GOD'S HOLY FORCE

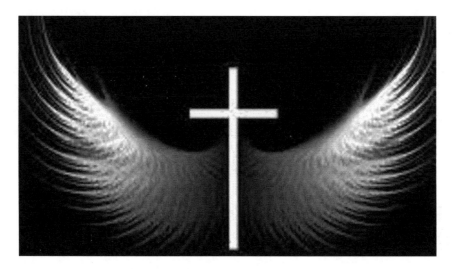

We have talked much about the Holy Spirit, God's holy Force, but now we will study about Him in depth. R.A. Torrey states, in The Person and Work of the Holy Spirit, that we must decide whether the "Holy Spirit is a divine Person, worthy of our adoration and our love; …and if He is some mysterious and wonderful power we can use; or who is a real person; holy, mighty, and tender who is to get a hold of and use us" (pg.9).

Personality characteristics such as knowledge, feelings, will, and teaching ability are ascribed to the Holy Spirit. Knowledge is ascribed to the Holy Spirit in 1 Corinthians 2:10-11, "The Spirit searches all things...The thoughts of God no one knows except the Spirit of God" (New American Standard Bible). Delegating and will are ascribed to the Holy Spirit in 1 Corinthians 12:11, which states that the Spirit distributes "to each one individually as He wills." Romans 15:30 talks about "the love of the Spirit," a feeling. Ephesians 4:30 says not to grieve the Holy Spirit, another feeling. John 14:26 states that, "The Holy Spirit...will teach you all things," which shows the personality characteristic of impartation of knowledge through <u>direct personal teaching</u>.

The Holy Spirit is indeed a Person, a distinct part of the Trinity, worthy to spend time with and learn of, as well as be praised and adored.

There are many jobs the Holy Spirit has that Scripture talks about: regeneration, conviction of sin, guidance, searching, and revealing, though that by no means encompasses all the works of the Spirit; God's Force here on earth. Please refer to the suggested reading list and bibliography for more information on the Holy Spirit.

Spiritual regeneration is the impartation of spiritual life to those who are spiritually dead because of their sins. Jesus said, "It is the Spirit who gives life" (John 6:63). Being regenerated is being "born again, not of corruptible seed, but incorruptible, through the Word of God" (1 Peter 1:23). When the Holy Spirit convicts you of your sin from the Scriptures and prompts you to receive Christ as your Lord and Savior, He comes to dwell within you permanently, in your new life. Conversion is the change from Satan's camp, the dark side, to God's camp, the righteous, light side. The outward manifestation of that internal work of regeneration is always evidenced by changed habits, changed lifestyles, joy, and peace (to name a few).

The Holy Spirit is your guidance counselor into all truth (John 16:13-14), and reveals even the depths of God (1 Corinthians 2:10). Acts 13:2 tells us the Holy Spirit separated Paul and Barnabas for a specific work and sent them out. So too, He can send you out, "for we are His workmanship, created in Christ Jesus for good works, which God prepared that we should walk in them" (Ephesians 2:10). How exactly the Holy Spirit called Paul and Barnabas in Acts 13:2 is silent, and so it is with you knowing God's will outside of what is clearly revealed in Scripture. He may make it known in one way and sometimes in another, but He will make His will known to you, if you ask Him to. Ask your Father in heaven, earnestly seek the answer, wait patiently upon the Lord for it, and expect God to speak through His Word, others, or His holy Force, the Holy Spirit in that still, small voice. Listen closely and desire nothing other than to fulfill God's will. **An absolutely surrendered will is imperative for your mind to be clear in God's will for you.** Otherwise, your will blocks Him from talking to you. How wonderful to be able to fulfill the good works that you were made for!

God also promises to provide all the guidance we need for every aspect of your life such as work, study, business, and relationships. James 1:5-7 states, "if any of you lacks wisdom, let him ask God, who gives to all liberally and without reproach … But let him ask in faith, with no doubting." So ask, without doubting!

God says that the Holy Spirit *indwells* each believer who has accepted Jesus Christ as their Lord and Savior. *Being filled* by the Spirit is something else. The filling of the Holy Spirit is the impartation of spiritual power for the sole purpose of testimony and service. God tells us His will in His Word, and the infilling of the Holy Spirit gives us the ability to carry it out. Dwight L moody wisely stated, "Before we pray that God would fill us, I believe we ought to pray for Him to empty us." So pray that way and watch God work!

Being filled with the Spirit is a command (Ephesians 5:18), so it cannot be something that happens only once and at salvation. What exactly is it? It is allowing "the Word of Christ dwell in you richly" (Colossians 3:16). God's power flows in your life and through you to others when you read, understand, and obey His Word. Go forth in the name of the Lord, knowing He has given you everything you need to finish the work He has called you to!

Scripture to memorize this week: Proverbs 23:12—"Apply your heart to instruction, and your ears to words of knowledge."

THE FLOW

The Holy Spirit dwells within us after we receive Christ as our Lord and Savior. Jesus said, "'If anyone thirsts, let him come to Me and drink. He who believes in Me, as the Scripture has said, out of his heart will flow rivers of living water.' But this He spoke concerning the Spirit, whom those believing in Him would receive" (John 7:37-39). This flow is the movement of love and God's Holy Spirit, His holy Force within us, directing and guiding our lives as we listen to Him.

The flow is within me,
Yet I don't follow.

I fear myself
That I will not trust myself
Enough to do what I hear.

Yet if I don't do what I hear,
It is wrong.
What a backward way!

But I know if I go with
The flow, I will know.

The fear is I may not
Be able to control myself.
That I will fall hard, care hard,
Love hard. Is that so bad?

It can be so good!

So what am I afraid of?

©nw

What doubts do you still have that God knows and loves you?

_____

_____

What fears do you have that prevent you from receiving this knowledge emotionally?

_____

_____

How have you seen God answer your prayers during the last few weeks?

_____

_____

What has been your pattern of spending time with God daily?

_____

_____

What will you have to sacrifice to make time for God?

_____

_____

_____

What changes would you want to make to spend more time alone with Him?

_____

_____

If you have done that already, what benefits have you received?

_____

_____

"O God, you are my God; early will I seek you," said the Psalmist (Psalm 63:1). If you follow his godly example, how much more will you have your antennae straight to hear God throughout the day! That will also help you set aside selfish motives resulting in better interaction patterns with others. How simple yet how hard to put into practice but practice makes almost perfect!

What fears do you have about the filling of the Holy Spirit and operating in God's holy Force?

_____

_____

What don't you understand about this filling?

_____

_____

If you don't understand the above, please find someone who is well versed in God's holy Force, the Holy Spirit, and walks with God and in His power.   Read the book, The Person and Work of the Holy Spirit, listed in the bibliography. Remember daily to ask for forgiveness of your sins, and then ask for God to fill you with His Force in obedience to His Word. We are weak and leaky vessels. God will fill you, for He always keeps his Word and delights in helping you obey all His commands if you are sincerely honest! In fact, "This is the confidence that we have in Him, that if we ask anything according to His will, He hears us [and in] whatever we ask [according to His revealed will], we know that we have the petitions that we have asked of Him" (1 John 5:14-15). If your heart attitude is right with God, ask whatever is according to His will as revealed in His word, and watch God's holy Force do much good through you!

⋏ ⋏ ⋏

12

SHARING THE FORCE WITH OTHERS

God's Principle: Discipleship

DISCIPLESHIP

DISCIPLESHIP IS SIMPLY teaching others what you have been taught. It is following in the footsteps of God's holy Force. You are a comforter who comes alongside others to support them in applying God's principles to their lives.

Effective discipleship calls for supporting, not rescuing or helping. The word help gives the impression that something is broken, or someone is incapable of doing something themselves. Rescuing is being overly protective and doing the work for the other person because they don't know how, or are thought to be inadequate. Rescuing prevents experiencing the consequences of actions taken and minimizes personal responsibility. As such, rescuing and helping are not God's way. God's way is for each believer to reach spiritual maturity, accepting responsibility for his or her own thoughts and actions. The spirit within the term support is assisting and encouraging the other person to be and do all that they were created to be and then, do.

The following is a tool to assist you in determining where you are in the supporting versus rescuing/helping roles that you play in your life. It is beneficial to be reflective and completely honest in your personal appraisal.

Mark each of the statements below as it applies to you according to the scoring code. The _____ stands for the significant others in your life: i.e., spouse, children, boss, parents, family, or friends.

SCORING CODE: 0 = seldom or never
1 = sometimes or occasionally
2 = frequently

1.   Is it hard for you to take time for yourself and have fun?   _____
2.   Do you supply words for _____ when he or she hesitates?   _____
3.   Do you set limits for yourself that you then ignore?   _____
4.   Do you believe you are responsible for making ____ happy?   _____
5.   Do you enjoy lending a shoulder for ____ to cry on?   _____
6.   Do you feel that others are not sufficiently grateful for your help?   _____
7.   Do you take care of others more than you take care of yourself?   _____
8.   Do you find yourself interrupting when ___ is talking?   _____
9.   Do you find it is difficult to say no to others?   _____
10. Do you make excuses, openly or mentally, for _____?   _____
11. Do you do more than your share or work harder than ____?   _____
12. When ____ is unsure or uncomfortable about doing something, do you take over?   _____
13. Do you give up doing things because ___wouldn't like it?   _____
14. Do you find yourself thinking that you really know what is best for
     than he or she does?   _____
15. Do you think ____ would have grave difficulty getting along without you?   _____
16. Do you use the word "we," and then find you don't have _____'s consent?   _____
17. Do you stop yourself by feeling ___ will feel badly if you say or do something?   _____
18. Is it hard for you not to respond to anyone who seems hurting or needing
     support, even when he or she does not ask?   _____
19. Do you find yourself giving advice that is not welcome?   _____
20. Do you find yourself being resented when you were only trying to be helpful?   _____
21. Is it easier to say 'I'll do it myself' rather than delegate appropriately to others?   _____

ADD UP YOUR POINTS:

                                                                              TOTAL_____

          0-10 = minimum rescuing
          11-19 = moderate rescuing
          20 + = extensive rescuing

Are you a rescuer? Are you a supporter? Look at the following examples of what support looks like vs. how a rescuer/ helper responds.

The following is a comparison of characteristics of both supporters and rescuers:

SUPPORTER

1. Listens for request
2. Presents offer
3. Gives only what is needed
4. Checks periodically with the person
5. Checks results:
    * functions better
    * meets goals
    * solves problems independently
    * uses suggestions successfully

RESCUER/HELPER

1. Gives when not asked
2. Neglects to find out if the offer is welcome
3. Gives help more and longer than needed
4. Omits feedback
5. Doesn't check results and feels good when accepted, but bad when turned down.

Many times people feel good by being helpful but project their own needs onto others because they are afraid to ask for what they really want. The result is a compulsive helper who never quite feels satisfied. This is done from the position of "I'm OK; you're not OK, so I have to step in and help you because you're so inadequate." These "rescuers" usually wind up being victims and are often persecuted by those they were trying to rescue. Have you experienced this?

You cannot change or support others unless they want to be changed or supported and then it is God who ultimately effects the change, not you. Truly supporting others can occur only when you are doing something for them that they desire and want. Giving support is more effective if you have been asked or received a "yes" if you asked whether support is wanted.

You may think that cultivating individual self-responsibility in others is selfish, uncaring, or callous. On the contrary, it is freedom to those who receive it. Realize also that you can most support others by going to God yourself for support. As He changes you, those around you will begin to respond to you differently. They have to! You are different and as an effect, they change also.

Refer to the supporter characteristics and what you have been learning in the past weeks to reach out to others and teach them what you know of God's way. May God bless your efforts!

Scripture to memorize this week: 2 Timothy 2:2—"The things that you have heard from me among many witnesses, commit these to faithful men who will be able to teach others also."

To share with others God's way, you must first be a disciple of God. A disciple is one who follows another's teachings and ways and shares with others. Obedience to His Word is key if you want His love and power to flow through you to others.

What does God say about restoring your brother in Galatians 6:1, which says, "If a man is overtaken in any trespass, you who are spiritual, restore such a one in a spirit of gentleness, considering yourself lest you also be tempted," and how does that apply to discipleship?

_____

_____

What does God say, in Galatians 6:9—"Let us not grow weary while doing good for in due season we shall reap if we do not lose heart," about the end product of our labors in discipleship?

_____

_____

What is God saying to you, in John 15:16—"You did not choose Me but I chose you, and appointed you that you should go and bear fruit…"

_____

_____

What fears do you have when you contemplate telling others what you have learned about God's way?

_____

Notice what Deuteronomy 31:8 tells us about God: "He is the One who goes before you. He will be with you, He will not leave you nor forsake you." How does that apply to your moving out in this?

_____

_____

Describe a recent scenario where you were telling someone what you have learned/are learning:

_____

_____

In knowing what to say as a disciple to others, notice what the Lord said to His most prominent disciple: "Who has made man's mouth? Or who makes the mute, the deaf, the seeing, or the blind? Have not I, the Lord? Now therefore, go, and I will be with your mouth and teach you what you shall say," Exodus 4:11. So even though you don't know everything, God can still use you if you are available and listening to His voice; not your own.

Therefore, Go with God and may He bless you with peace.

▲ ▲ ▲

SUGGESTED READING LIST

The following are secular books that may be helpful, but read them with caution and a biblically discerning mind.

Beattie, Melody. (1987). Codependent No More. New York: Harper & Row.

Bradshaw, John. (1988). The Family. Florida: Health Communications, Inc.

Fromm, Erich. (1956). The Art of Loving. New York: Harper & Row.

Peck, M. Scott, MD. (1978). The Road Less Traveled. New York: Simon & Schuster, Inc.

The following list is from a more Christian perspective. I encourage you to read especially Francis Schaeffer's, True Spirituality, R.A. Torry's, The Person and Work of the Holy Spirit, and J. Keith Miller's, A Hunger for Healing.

Bennett, Dennis and Rita. (1971). The Holy Spirit and You. New Jersey: Logos International.

Bridges, Jerry. (1978). The Pursuit of Holiness. Colorado: Navpress.

Bridges, Jerry. (1983). The Practice of Godliness. Colorado: Navpress.

Buhler, Rich. (1988). Pain and Pretending. Tennessee: Thomas Nelson, Inc.

Esses, Michael. (1974). The Phenomenon of Obedience. New Jersey: Logos International.

Huggett, Joyce. (1986). The Joy of Listening to God. Illinois: InterVarsity Press.

Miller, J. Keith. (1991). A Hunger for Healing. New York: Harper Collins.

Powell, John. (1969). Why Am I Afraid to Tell You Who I Am?. Illinois: Argus Communications.

Powell, John. (1974). The Secret of Staying in Love. Texas: Argus Communications.

Powell, John. (1976). Fully Human, Fully Alive. Illinois: Argus Communications.

Powell, John. (1978). Unconditional Love. Texas: Argus Communications.

Schaeffer, Francis A. (1971). True Spirituality. Illinois: Tyndale House Publishers.

Seamands, David A. (1981). Healing for Damaged Emotions. Illinois: SP Publications, Inc.

Smalley, Gary and Trent, John, Ph.D. (1986), The Blessing. Tennessee: Thomas Nelson, Inc.

Smith, Chuck. (1979,1980). Effective Prayer Life. California: The Word For Today.

Swindoll, Charles R. (1983). Dropping Your Guard. New York: Bantam Books.

Torrey, R.A. (1974). The Person & Work of the Holy Spirit (rev. ed.). Michigan: Zondervan Publishing House.

Watson, David. (1980). The Hidden Battle. Illinois: Harold Shaw Publishers.

Whitfield, Charles L., M.D. (1987). Healing the Child Within. Florida: Health Communications, Inc.

Wilkerson, David; and Sherrill, John & Elizabeth. (1963). The Cross and The Switchblade. New Jersey: Spire Books.

⋏ ⋏ ⋏

APPENDIX

CONTENTS

Using *A Way of Life* in Group Settings 97

Dependence on God 99

Perfect Love 100

Daily Acceptance Prayer 101

Confrontation and Communication 102

How We Learn and Communicate 105

Communication 106

Guidelines in Handling Certain Situations .111

Word Pictures 111

Listening 113

Please Hear What I'm Not Saying 115

Stress Management 116

The Social Readjustment Rating Scale 120

Tithing 123

Year at-A-Glance 125

Decision Making/Problem-Solving Process 128

Life Philosophy 131

Goal Setting 134

Life Domain Goals 136

The Grief Process 139

The First and Second Greatest Commandments 141

The Ten Commandments 142

My Praise Song 143

The Way It Is Meant To Be 144

Dear Little One, ...145

Serenity Prayer 146

Come, Child of My Love 147

Bibliography 149

USING *A WAY OF LIFE* IN GROUP SETTINGS

This book has been used in multiple group settings, so the below has been included to support group success and encourage individuals to be facilitators. Usually there is sharing of what God is doing in each person and what spoke to them in the chapter being reviewed.

GROUP LEADERS

Ground Rules, which are to be read to the small group:

- Confidentiality is of utmost importance.
- Please don't put down another's person, thoughts, or opinions—each person is of equal value.
- It's OK to say that you don't want to share.
- Please share time equally. Give everyone a chance to share.
- One person talks at a time.
- Please be personal. Use "I" or "me" statements.
- We work together as a team.
- Talk from feelings, not stories or circumstances.
- Don't give advice.
- Listen and try to understand what is being said.

Good Family Functional Rules taken from Bradshaw on: The Family by John Bradshaw. Copyright 1988. Health Communications, Inc. Used with permission from the author.

- Problems are acknowledged and resolved.
- 5 freedoms—can be expressed and explored:
    - perceptions
    - feelings
    - thoughts
    - desires
    - fantasies
- Communication is direct, specific, and behavioral.
- Family members get their needs met.
- Family members can be different.
- Parents do what they say (self-disciplined disciplinarians).
- Atmosphere is fun and spontaneous.
- The rules require accountability.
- Violation of another's values leads to guilt.
- Mistakes are forgiven and viewed as learning tools.
- Individuals are in touch with their healthy shame.
- The family systems exist for each other.

What to discuss in the group setting:

- What was particularly meaningful to you from the last chapter?
- How do you see this affecting your life right now?
- Are there any changes that you want to make?

Closing in Prayer:

If anyone wants prayer, what can we pray about for you tonight or during this coming week?

DEPENDENCE ON GOD

Draw a circle, where God is in the middle, and all the following points have their focus on Him, and His way. Do this and you will live!

The beginning of your dependence on God starts with your Willingness, and goes until you BE, DO, and then, Have.

Point # 1	You are WILLING
Point # 2	You are SINCERE
Point # 3	You ASK TO BE SHOWN
Point # 4	You are AWARE
Point # 5	You ACCEPT WHAT WE ARE SHOWN
Point # 6	You TAKE THE ISSUE TO GOD
Point # 7	You ASK TO BE CHANGED
Point # 8	You EXPECT A CHANGE
Point # 9	You look for what ACTION TO TAKE
Point # 10	You TAKE THE ACTION, then
Point # 11	You BE, DO, then HAVE

To refresh the understanding of what is meant by the BE—DO—HAVE statement, refer to the preface at the beginning of this book. Then, enjoy and experience the new found freedom, which is given to you as you submit and depend on God!

PERFECT LOVE

Everyone longs to give himself or herself completely to someone: To have a deep, soul relationship with another, to be loved thoroughly and exclusively. But to you, Christian, I say no. Not until you're satisfied and fulfilled and content with being loved by Me alone, and giving yourself totally and unreservedly to Me in an intensely personal and unique relationship with Me. I love you, My child, and until you discover that only in Me is your fullest satisfaction to be found, you will not be capable of the perfect human relationship that I have planned for you.

You will never be united with another until you are united with Me, exclusive of any other desires or longings. I want you to stop planning, stop wishing, and allow Me to bless you in My time. You just keep watching Me, expecting the greatest things. Keep learning and listening to the things I tell you. You must wait.

Don't be anxious, looking around at the things you think you want. Just keep looking up to Me, or you'll miss what I have to show you.

Then, when you're ready, I'll surprise you with a love far more wonderful than any you would ever dream. You see, until you are ready and until the one I have for you is ready, I am working this minute to have both of you ready at the same time, and until you are both satisfied exclusively with Me and the life I've prepared for you, you won't be able to experience the perfect love that exemplifies your relationship with Me.

And dear one, I want you to have this most wonderful love. I want you to personally experience a picture of your relationship with Me, enjoying materially and concretely the everlasting union of beauty, perfection, and love that I offer you with Myself. Know that I love you with an everlasting love. I am God Almighty; believe and be satisfied.

Always,

Your Heavenly Father

▲ ▲ ▲

Daily Acceptance Prayer

Acceptance is the answer to all my problems today—

When I'm disturbed, it is because I feel some person, place, thing, or situation is unacceptable to me.

I can find no serenity until I accept that person, place, thing, or situation as being exactly the way it is supposed to be at this moment.

Nothing happens in God's world by mistake.

Until I accept responsibility for my attitudes, I cannot have peace in my life.

Unless I accept life completely on life's terms, I cannot be happy.

I get to concentrate not so much on what needs to be changed in the world around me as on what needs to be changed in my attitudes and in me.

Thank You, Lord, for the day You have made.

Author unknown

▲ ▲ ▲

CONFRONTATION AND COMMUNICATION
Confrontation is not an ugly word!

The Apostle Paul explained to the Ephesian church, "All things that are exposed are made manifest by the light, for whatever makes manifest is light" (Ephesians 5:13). The Word of God is your source of light. God's principles are there to guide you in how to interact with your fellow human beings, separating truth from error.   He gives you His holy Force to support you in discerning the truth from the lie.

Confrontation is not an ugly word. It can be used to set God's people free when the truth is spoken in love. You can be set free yourself by standing on the truth, and speaking it. Denial can be broken. In order to deny, individuals are required to be dishonest. Satan would love for the fog in your mind to become increasingly thick. Then, you will have a hard time hearing God OR seeing Him move in your life. Denial is a sin. You likely use it to protect yourself for one reason or another, but it is time to put to death that method of hiding from others and yourself and bring all aspects of your life to the light of God's Word. Confrontation is basically speaking the truth, or what you perceive to be truth, until the full picture is known (knowing that you may not have all the facts available to you). It is bringing what was hidden to the light. It is a way of working with others, being sensitive to them as fellow creatures of God, as you verbalize the truth. The Holy Spirit, God's holy Force, is your guide for sensitivity regarding if, when, and how you are to speak.

Motives are to be evaluated prior to any confrontation with another. Operating in anger or revenge is not following the principles of God. An attitude of looking for the best, and desiring for the truth to reign gracefully, is a must in how you interact with another. Our MOTIVE must be one of LOVE.

Communication is an art. It is active listening, coupled with discernment and sensitivity. Active listening is tuning into the actual words, as well as any underlying messages (undercurrents). Many individuals say they are fine, but really are not. What they usually want is for someone else (you?) to take the initiative to ask them what is wrong. If that occurs, a need is met. If not, the individual goes away feeling as if no one cares about them, which is a lie. Was there truthful communication there? No. This occurs frequently in relationships. We expect other individuals to read our minds, and when they don't, we blame them for not meeting our needs. Who is really to blame? We are, because we were not clear in communicating our needs. That is why WORDS and HOW WE USE THEM are so important. "Death and life are in the power of the tongue, and those who love it will eat its fruit" (Proverbs 18:21). One of those fruits is bridging the gap between separation and intimacy. Remember, be kind, direct, and clear.

Thoughtful questioning is another ingredient in the confrontation and communication process to clarify what is heard. What one individual means with a word may be different from your perception of that word. Clarify so you both can be sure you are talking the same language. Have you ever walked away from a conversation feeling uncertain about what was decided? Avoid that by being direct and clear.

Write down an example of a sensitive issue that you talked over with someone:

_____

_____

_____

Do you feel that you had the issue clearly defined in your mind prior to the conversation?

_____

What was your attitude prior to the communication?

_____

_____

Do you feel that what you were trying to communicate was done clearly or vaguely?

_____

What was good about how the communication worked out?

_____

_____

What could have been improved?

_____

_____

How did you feel before you began talking?

_____

_____

How did you feel after the conversation was over?

_____

_____

Do you feel that the truth was established?

_____

Why or why not?

_____

_____

In communication that requires confrontation, how another responds to your communication is not the issue. God calls you to be honest and righteous before Him. If your heart is pure before Him, as you communicate necessary and/or difficult issues with another person, the outcome is up to the other individual before Him. You are responsible only for your actions and attitudes. How the other responds is his or her responsibility before God and there will be times when such communication works wonderfully well, and intimacy is established. How joyful are those times! However, there will be times of sorrow and confusion when difficult conversations do not end well. Evaluate your part in why the outcome happened the way that it did, and learn from your mistakes. God loves you just the way you are, but because of His love for you, He doesn't want you to stay there. He wants to transform you to be like Him, and will use even difficult conversations to help bring that about.

How We Learn and Communicate

Most of us fall into one of the following categories of learning and communicating. As you seek to relate well to one another, it is helpful to be aware of how you and those you are communicating with learn or hear best. You can then learn to talk in their "language." The description of each separate category concludes with examples to enhance our ability to communicate with this type of learner.

Visual:

This person learns and communicates best through sight. Using word pictures helps get the message across to him or her. This is drawing, with words, a visual illustration of what you are trying to say. Using words such as watch, look, gaze, reflect, see, and show tap into this sight activity. (We will consider this further in a separate section.)

> Examples:
>> "I see what you mean."
>> "It looks OK to me."
>> "This appears to be right to me."

Auditory:

This person learns and communicates best through hearing. You can identify an auditory learner by the words he or she uses such as hear, say, sound, talk, tell, and explain.

> Examples:
>> "Do you hear what I am saying?"
>> "Let me tell you."
>> "Does that ring a bell?"
>> "It sounds interesting to me."

Kinesthetic:

This person learns and communicates best through being able to touch, taste, smell, chew, hold, and feel things. He or she learns best through experience. A kinesthetic learner is likely to use words such as build, feel, catch, do, grasp, hold, make, shape, and touch.

> Examples:
>> "That feels good to me."
>> "I think I can grasp that."

The following example shows the difference in language between the three categories:

Visual:	"That looks good to me."
Auditory:	"That sounds good to me."
Kinesthetic:	"That feels good to me."

We all operate in all three categories, but each of us normally favor one category over another. Knowing how you and those closest to you tend to communicate will promote peaceful relationships as you talk to them in their favorite learning and communicating language!

COMMUNICATION

The following depicts key elements of the communication process. They are given in outline fashion to make it easy for you to review them often, for the more you understand and practice them, the more your communication with others will improve.

Communicate with purpose:

- Influence behavior/ideas/thoughts.
- Convey information.
- Build relationships.

Before communicating, ask yourself if your purpose is to confront, resolve an issue, or share since the way you approach speaking will differ. Remember a key biblical concept: Philippians 2:3—"Let nothing be done through selfish ambition or conceit, but in lowliness of mind let each esteem others better than himself." Applying that scripture to our attitude and heart as we communicate will support our awareness of how our words may be perceived by others, and how that affects their feelings.

Ways of communicating:

- Linear-----one sided.
        person A sends message to person B
        sender-------->--------->receiver
- Circular.
        person A sends message to B and B responds and feedback happens
        sender A <------------->B receiver and then sender
- Mutual transaction.
        person A sends message to B, B responds, and A then responds
                A----->B----->A----->B
        feedback happens both ways, increased emotional relating (both influence the other)

Sender:

- Must be clear in message sent.
- Responsible to evaluate the words used to send the message.

Receiver:

- Responsible to understand that they hear through their perception filter, which can result in a different message heard than what was sent.

Be aware that receivers can have preconceived ideas of the sender, which will cloud communication. Mutual transaction helps ensure that what was said was heard correctly.

Non-verbal communication:

Non-verbal communication comprises about 55 percent of the communication process. The rest of the breakdown is 7 percent verbal, 38 percent vocal, with inconsistencies in what we say and do frequently occurring.

a. All 5 senses are used.
b. 4 categories.
- Kinesics—body movements, facial expressions, body language, clothes.
- Tactile—who can touch whom, when, and how.
- Paralanguage—how voice is when speaking.
- Proxemics.
  - Use of physical/personal space.
  - Who can come in and when.
  - Distance.
    - public—no personal contact
    - social—4-12 feet
    - personal—1½ -4 feet
    - intimate—6"-18"
c. More feelings are communicated non-verbally than verbally.

Factors affecting how communication is perceived:

a. Mood.
b. Preconceived notions of the speaker and the topic being spoken about (selective hearing).
c. Mental level of the person being spoken to.

Evaluating your communication:

a. Speaker—primary responsibility to get ideas across.
- Emotions can cloud the words used.
- Emotions cloud the way words are used.
- Pushing past emotion, speak accurately and lovingly.
- Stay focused and avoid distractions.
b. Hearer—keep in mind:
- Distractions.
- Vocabulary and language skills.
- Wishful hearing.
- Perception filter.
c. Things to avoid in your communication:
- Using clichés.
- Giving unwanted advice or approval.

- Belittling speech or actions.
- Disagreeably disagreeing.
- Being defensive.
- Stereotyping and over-generalizing.
- Changing the subject before resolution.
- Blaming.
- Responding with anger and hostility—Proverbs 17:14 says, "The beginning of strife is like a releasing [a flood]. Therefore stop contention before a quarrel starts."
- Raising more than one issue at a time.
- Judging (condemning) —Matthew 7:2—"With what judgment you judge, you will be judged."

Tools for good communication:

a. Active listening—we speak about 125 words per minute, but think about 4 times as fast.
- Demonstrate understanding and respect for the speaker's message and feelings.
- Be empathetic and sympathetic.
- Concentrate on the speaker's perspective.
- Is not casual—takes energy.
- Is not parroting back words, but using open-ended questions, such as, "Can you give me an example?"
- Is a priority: James 1:19 says, "Let every man be swift to hear, slow to speak, slow to wrath."
b. Considerate speaking:
- Raise only one issue at a time.
- "Be kind to one another, tenderhearted to one another, just as God in Christ forgave you" (Ephesians 4:32).
- "A soft answer turns away wrath, but a harsh word stirs up anger" (Proverbs 15:1).
- Proverbs 16:21 says, "The wise in heart will be called prudent, and sweetness of the lips increases learning."
c. Clarification:
- Attempt to understand.
- Validate what a person is saying.
- Focus.
- Summarize to make sure what was said was indeed heard.
d. Be aware of others and your nonverbal body language (see following pages).
e. Follow the speaker—Jesus told His disciples to follow and learn of Him; to learn of His perspective. With following skills, we can walk alongside others and learn their perspective.

Concluding scriptural consideration: Philippians 4:8 says to meditate on whatever is:

- True.
- Noble.
- Just.
- Pure.
- Lovely.

- Of good reputation.
- Virtuous.
- Praise worthy.

God calls us to cultivate an attitude of thinking the best for all and facilitating the best in all. Our flesh wants us to assume the worst, even though the worst may not exist except in our own mind because of our past. God calls us not to think on those things but on the best, so training our minds is our ongoing task.

NON-VERBAL BEHAVIORAL COMPONENTS

Type	Aggressive	Assertive	Passive
Eye contact	stares, glares	looks in eyes	avoids eyes
Posture	exaggerated, rigid	open, upright	slumped, head down
Gestures	tightly clenched fist, points finger	relaxed, expressive	fidgeting hands
Distance	intrusive	comfortable	moves away
Verbal loudness	louder than normal range	normal range	softer than normal range
Tone of voice	harsh	clear	clear to sing-song/whiny
Style/fluency	offensive, bombastic	direct, smooth	indirect, interrupts
Content	derogatory put-downs	to the point, brief	wordy, indirect
Listening	interrupts, closed to other's viewpoint	doesn't interrupt when others speak, listens to others viewpoint, open	tendency is to partially listen to what is said, often misinterprets

BASICS OF GOOD COMMUNICATION
- Active listening
- Open questioning
- Accepting and reflecting feelings

Principle	Examples of Active Listening
Convey interest in what the other person is saying	Smiling, nodding, eye contact, "I see," "Uh-huh"
Encourage the other to expand further	"Yes, go on," "Tell me more," "I'd like to hear more"
Help the other clarify the problem in their thinking	"Then the problem as you see it is that…"
Help the other hear what they have said, in the say it sounded to you	"If I understand you correctly, you are saying that…"
Pull out the key ideas	"Your major concern is…"
Respond to the other's feelings more than their words	"You feel strongly that…"

GUIDELINES IN HANDLING CERTAIN SITUATIONS

Offering constructive compliments

- Be specific—focus on behavior or incident.
- Be direct.
- Compliment in public.
- Compliment often, but be sincere and sensitive.

Offering constructive criticism

- Be specific—focus on a behavior or incident.
- Be sure the behavior you are criticizing can be changed.
- Talk from your own point of view, and avoid threats and accusations.
- Don't belabor the point.
- Offer incentives for changed behavior, and commit yourself to share in resolving the situation.
- Empathize with the other's problem or feelings.
- Choose an appropriate time and place.

Accepting compliments

- Say thank you!

Accepting criticism

- Think of it as a source of new information to be evaluated objectively.
- Channel the emotional energy aroused by criticism into fruitful avenues.
- Take the necessary steps to put behavioral changes into action.

WORD PICTURES

The following was borrowed from the book The Language of Love by Gary Smalley and John Trent, Ph.D., and published by Focus on the Family. © 1988. All rights reserved. International copyright secured. Used by permission from Focus on the Family.

What word pictures are:

They are a communication tool that uses a story or object to simultaneously activate the emotions and intellect of a person. This, in turn, causes a person to experience our words, not just hear them. The impact of our words is multiplied. A word picture usually does not have a literal meaning. It is a coloring book in words.

Reasons why word pictures work:

- Time-tested by world's greatest communicators.
  - Aristotle—"He entered combat in body like the strongest bull, in spirit like the fiercest lion."
  - Churchill—"Dictators may walk to and fro among tigers, but they dare not be deceived. The tigers are getting hungry, too." (Cautionary note regarding word pictures: Dictators use them too, so beware of the motive of the speaker.)
  - Martin Luther King, Jr. —"Let us not seek to satisfy our thirst for freedom by drinking from the cup of bitterness and hatred."
  - Excerpts from the Bible—Psalm 23 and the Good Shepherd, Luke 10 and the Good Samaritan.
- Grab and direct attention (first 30 seconds is most important).
  - Only have a few seconds to really get someone's attention. We don't drive cars—we drive Mustangs, Broncos.
  - Our brain works faster with pictures than listening to conventional words, which promotes straining to see what lies behind the story.
- Brings the message to life.
  - Activates emotions that can produce a positive change in one's thinking.
  - Creates a theater of the mind or mental journey.
  - Can be physically affecting, triggering all 5 senses.
- Lock thoughts into our memory: not a lost memory, but a lasting memory.
- Gateway to intimacy.
  - Bridges the gap between the different ways of thinking between men and women.
  - Women use 25,000 words/day; tells the story first, then facts. telling the story first helps a woman attempt to get a man to feel and hear her words, and maximizes her innate relational abilities.
  - Men use 12,500 words/day; wants facts first, then the story.

How to create a word picture:

- Establish clear purposes.
  - Motivate godly and noble resolve.
  - Clarify thoughts and feelings.
  - Move to a deeper intimacy level.
  - Praise or encourage someone.
  - Lovingly correct someone.
- Study the other person's interest.
  - David—shepherd/defender word pictures.
  - Paul—athlete/laborer word pictures.
- Draw from the following 4 inexhaustible wells.
  - Nature and its wonders—e.g., woods, birds.
  - Everyday objects—e.g., leftovers, flags.
  - Imaginary stories—can be memorable; e.g., Narnia, Middle Earth.
  - Past experiences and remembrances—direct path to a person's emotions.

- Rehearse your story.
- Give it at the right time and place.

The value of using word pictures in the home:

- Security—creating a warm blanket of love.
  - Score with family members from 1-10 on how secure they feel. A score of 1 would not be very secure and a 10 score would be very secure.
  - Discern what it would take to move closer or maintain the security level.
  - Use word pictures to strengthen the self-esteem of each family member.
- Meaningful communication—heart to heart praise, discipline, love.
- Psalm 128 family word picture: "Blessed is everyone who fears the Lord, who walks in His ways. When you eat the labor of your hands, you shall be happy, and it shall be well with you. Your wife shall be like a fruitful vine in the very heart of your house, your children like olive plants all around your table. Behold, thus shall the man be blessed who fears the Lord" (vv.1-4).

LISTENING
Listen to Understand:

- Love looks to understand.
- Understanding promotes love and intimacy.
- Promote an attitude of looking for the truth to really listen and understand.
- With knowledge comes understanding.

PROVERBS ON UNDERSTANDING:

Proverbs 2:2-3 states—"Incline your ear to wisdom, and apply your heart to understanding; yes, if you cry out for discernment, and lift up your voice for understanding ...then you will understand the fear of the Lord, and find the knowledge of God."

Proverbs 4:5—"Get wisdom! Get understanding!"

Proverbs 13:15-16—"Good understanding gains favor.... Every prudent man acts with knowledge, but a fool lays open his folly."

Proverbs 16:22—"Understanding is a wellspring of life to him who has it."

PROVERBS ON SPEAKING THE TRUTH:

Proverbs 12:17,22—"He who speaks truth declare righteousness. ...Those who deal truthfully are His delight."

Proverbs 15:28—"The heart of the righteous studies how to answer, but the mouth of the wicked pours forth evil."

A BLESSING FOR THE LISTENER

With your ear, may you hear each word as something very precious.
With your mind, may you humbly search to understand.
With your eye, may you note the non-verbal message.
With your heart, may you listen with real love.
And may your hearing, understanding, and loving be as lasting and enduring as a precious stone.

PLEASE HEAR WHAT I'M NOT SAYING

Don't be fooled by the face I wear, for I wear a mask. I wear many masks, masks I'm afraid to take off, and none of them are I.

Pretending is an art that is second nature to me, but don't be fooled. I give you the impression I am secure. That confidence is my name, and coolness is my game. That the water is calm, and I'm in command needing no one. But—please don't believe that.

My surface may be smooth, but my surface is my mask. Beneath dwells the real me, in confusion, fear, and aloneness. But I hide that. I don't want anyone to know it. I panic at the thought of my weakness and fear being exposed. That's why I frantically create a mask to hide behind: a nonchalant, sophisticated facade to help me pretend, to shield me from the glance that knows. But—such a glance is my only salvation, and I know it. That is, if it is followed by acceptance and love. It is the only thing that can liberate me from myself, from the barriers I so painstakingly erect. It is the only thing that will assure me of what I can't assure myself: that I really am worth something.

I'd really like to be genuine, but please help me. Please hold out your hands, even when that's the last thing I seem to want or need. Only you can call me into aliveness. Each time you're kind, gentle, and encouraging: each time you try to understand because you really care, you breathe life into me. I want you to know that. I want you to know how important you are to me. You can be a creator of the person I am becoming if you choose to be. You can help break down the wall behind which I tremble. You can help release me from the lonely prison of panic and insecurity. Please don't pass me by. It will not be easy. A long-time conviction of worthlessness builds strong walls. The nearer you approach me, the more likely I will strike back. I know it's irrational, but at times, I am irrational. I fight against the very thing I cry out for. But I am told that love is stronger than strong walls, and there lies my hope—my only hope.

Please break down these walls with gentle hands, for I am very sensitive. Who am I? I am someone you know very well: I am every person you'll ever meet.

Anonymous

⊼ ⊼ ⊼

STRESS MANAGEMENT

Stress is an ever-present reality. Some of us thrive on or even create more stress in our lives, while others run from any kind of stress. Stress can be either positive or negative. The key to managing stress in a healthy way is the tools we use to cope with it.

Stress is any strain or pressure on the body or mind. A stressor is that which causes stress. Distress is a state of mental or physical anguish. It can also be the result of mismanaged stress. Recognizing the kind of stress we are under as well as our usual response to stress is how we begin managing the stress in our lives.

PHYSICAL SYMPTOMS OF DISTRESS:

Anxiety	Churning stomach	Depression
Edginess	Poor concentration	Short-temperedness
Irritability	Accelerated speech	Tight shoulders
Sore back	Fuzzy thinking	Hand trembling

There may be other symptoms that your body manifests. Write these in the space provided:

_____

_____

_____

_____

_____

The above symptoms are some of the early warning signs that something is wrong and needs to be changed. Doctors estimate that approximately 80 percent of illnesses are stress-related. The following are sometimes the manifestations of chronically ignored stress (by no means indicating that if you have one of these diseases, it was necessarily because of chronic stress):

Ulcers	Heart attacks
Cancer	Rheumatoid arthritis
High-blood pressure	Dizziness
Migraine headaches	Chronic back pain
Colitis	Non-cardiac pain

Our performance level can tell us our stress level. If we are too busy and don't have time to carry out our normal responsibilities, our body will let us know. Our energy level will begin to drop and our focus as believers on God's will begins to wane. Conversely, not having enough stress in our lives can be as bad as having too much.

INDICATORS OF IDEAL STRESS LEVEL

High-energy level	Thorough analysis of problems
Mental alertness	Improved memory and recall
High motivation	Sharp perception
Calmness under pressure	Optimistic outlook

INDICATORS OF UNDER-STRESS OR OVER-STRESS

Boredom	Fatigue
Apathy	Insomnia
High accident rate	Change in appetite
Frequent grievances	Negative outlook
Absenteeism	Errors/indecisiveness
Increased use of drugs, alcohol, food, or tobacco	

FIGHT-OR-FLIGHT RESPONSE

When stress enters, our baseline stress level rises and then falls with the resolution of the stress. If our stress is chronic, our baseline rises, but does not fall back to its normal level. That taxes the chemical structure of our body on an ongoing basis, with the eventual breakdown somewhere in our mind or body.

MANAGING STRESS

An integrated approach to managing stress is vital to the proper care of the person God made you to be.

EQUIPPING YOUR SPIRIT

From what I have seen in my life and by observing others, the primary cause of negative stress (distress) is the desire for control. Prayer is a wonderful remedy, as it brings us before our Father in our rightful place of submission as His children. When we "seek first the kingdom of God and His righteousness" (Matthew 6:33), control ceases to be important. I have felt the tension leave me as I tell Him of my concerns and struggles, and leave them in His hands.

EQUIPPING YOUR MIND

Taking time each day to relax and allow our bodies to quiet down is important for turning off the fight-or-flight response. So also are learning to put limits and saying no to external and internal demands. Jesus said to His disciples, "Come aside...and rest awhile" (Mark 6:31). We need periodic rest and renewal to keep ourselves at peak efficiency. Rest also helps us to regroup and focus—to make sure we are going in the direction our Maker intended us to go rather than aimlessly being active. Bringing all thoughts into the captivity of Jesus (2 Corinthians 10:5), will enable us to determine what voice we are hearing. If it does not line up with the Word, the voice may be our flesh or Satan. Another helpful scripture to monitor our minds is Philippians 4:8, which states, "Whatever things are true...noble...just...pure...lovely...of good report; if there is any virtue, and if there is anything praiseworthy—think on these things." Applying this scripture is the death of thoughts as "I'm no good," "No one loves me," "I'm a failure." God says to "be transformed by the renewing of your mind" (Romans 12:2—to look and see what I, God, think of you and for you to know Me). Learning and accepting how God thinks and promises to act towards us is key to winning the battle of the mind. It is a conscious battle. To win, we must take the responsibility for disciplining our own thoughts.

EQUIPPING YOUR BODY

Regular physical exercise is important for a number of reasons, including:

- Healthy outlet for stored energy.
- Increases circulation and improves body functions.
- Increases production of endorphins for feelings of well being.
- Increases muscle tissue.

Regular exercise keeps our body strong so that at times of strain, we will not hurt ourselves. Regular exercise raises our metabolism rate by increasing muscle tissue, which burn calories more efficiently than fat tissue. Fad diets do not work. If your goal is to lose weight, increase your amount of exercise, and cut down the fat content of the food you are eating. Over a period of time, if you are consistent, your weight will start to drop. For women, regular exercise that places stress on our long bones helps build them up and counteracts the effects of osteoporosis.

In looking at stress management, many of us do not even consider what we do to our bodies when we consume the foods that we do. How does our body react to certain foods? How hard does our body have to work to digest one food over another? Is our mind clearer when we eat certain foods than others? Caffeine and sugar play a major part in increasing stress. Caffeine stimulates our kidneys and if consumed in excess, can cause increased nervous symptoms. Caffeine also depletes the body of our stress vitamins by increasing our urinary output and as Vitamins B and C are water soluble, they are excreted through the kidneys via urine. Eating a high-sugar diet depletes the stress vitamins in our bodies (Vitamins B and C), while shocking our pancreas when a load of sugar is pumped into the bloodstream. As the pancreas responds with a release of insulin, if no protein is around to stabilize the blood sugar, the blood sugar will initially shoot up and we feel a rush of energy. A short time later, because of the amount of insulin released, our blood sugar will drop and we can become listless, tired, and depressed. So we eat again and the roller coaster continues. Two excellent books for more information on nutrition are The Nutrition Almanac and Dr. Roger T. Williams Nutrition Against Disease (both are listed in the bibliography).

Other stress-management tools include:

- Social support—Allow family, friends, church and neighbors to lend stability, guidance, and caring to your life. Strength flows from giving as well as receiving.
- Anchors—Be faithful to follow your religious and personal beliefs, establish sensible daily routines, and identify a few favorite spots in nature both near and far you like to spend time at.
- Physical care—Continue good health and fitness habits during both good and bad times. Make priorities of eating well, exercising, and relaxing.
- Involvement—Get involved. Active participation in the community, church, and political affairs adds to a sense of belonging and contribution to others. Don't wait for others to come to you—go to them.
- Perception—Have God's worldview, as well as God's perception of who you are: His valued child.
- Reactions to distress—Make choices and decisions in a timely manner with godly counsel rather than ignoring the issues you know you need to face.

The ways I normally react to stress are:

_____

_____

_____

_____

The areas in my life right now with the most stress are:

_____

_____

I want to make the following changes in my lifestyle:

_____

_____

I will incorporate these tools by:

_____

_____

_____

THE SOCIAL READJUSTMENT RATING SCALE

Drs. Thomas Holmes and Richard Rahe of the Department of Psychiatry at the University of Washington School of Medicine developed the Social Readjustment Rating Scale. This scale, originally published in the Journal of Psychosomatic Research Volume 11 (1967), is reprinted with permission from Elsevier Science Ltd., Pergamom Imprint, Oxford, England, and lists forty-three life events along with a corresponding value. A person's score on this scale can be useful in predicting that person's chances of becoming ill or having an accident in the next two years. **A score of 150 to 299 indicates approximately a 50-percent chance; a score of above 300 indicates approximately a 90-percent chance of becoming seriously ill or injured in the next two years.** This research indicates a strong correlation between stress and illness, but also illustrates that people react differently to stressors. If stressors alone caused illness, then 100-percent of those with high scores would become ill. If you have a high score on this scale, that doesn't mean you are going to become ill. It means it's time to use your resources and strengths to minimize your chances and take extra good care of yourself.

To use this rating scale, add the value of each life event that applies to you within the last year, and total your score.

LIFE EVENT	SCORE
Death of a spouse	100
Divorce	73
Marital separation	65
Jail term	63
Death/family member	63
Personal injury/illness	53
Marriage	50
Fired at work	47
Marital reconciliation	45
Retirement	45
Health	44
Pregnancy	40
Change in family members	39
Sex difficulties	39
Gain of new family member	39
Business readjustment	39
Change in financial state	38
Death of a close friend	37
Change of line of work	36
Change in number of arguments with spouse	35
Mortgage or loan. A major purchase	31
Foreclosure of mortgage or loan	30
Change in responsibility at work	29
Son or daughter leaves home	29
Trouble with in-laws	29
Outstanding personal achievement	28
Begin or end school	26
Wife begins or stops work	26
Change in living conditions	25
Revision of personal habits	24
Trouble with the boss	23
Change/work hrs/conditions	20
Change in residence	20
Change in schools	20
Change in recreation	19
Change in church activities	19
Change in social activities	18
Mortgage/loan for a lesser purchase	17
Change in sleeping habits	16
Change in eating habits	15
Change in # of family get-togethers	15
Vacation	13
Minor violation of the law	11

TOTAL: _____

What other events can you think of in your life that are not listed in this scale took significant energy for you to adjust to?

_____

_____

What coping skills do you see already incorporated in your life?

_____

_____

_____

What coping skills do you plan to incorporate into your life and how do you plan to do that?

_____

_____

_____

▲ ▲ ▲

TITHING

In seeking to be good stewards of the finances God has given us, we will start with the topic of tithing. What is tithing, and what is taught about it in Scripture?

The term "tithe" means a tenth and yet it is hardly the last word on all God's principles regarding giving. Here is a basic summary using the following scriptures taken from the Old Testament:

Genesis 28:22—Jacob said to God, "Of all that You give me, I will surely give a tenth [tithe] to You."

Leviticus 27:32—"Concerning the tithe of the herd…the tenth one shall be holy to the Lord." The tithe was a part of the Levitical law given to the nation of Israel.

Ecclesiastes 5:4-5—"When you make a vow to God, do not delay to pay it….Better not to vow than to vow and not pay."

The following scriptures are taken from the New Testament:

Matthew 6:1-4—"Do not do your charitable deed before men, to be seen by them….Do…in secret; and your Father who sees in secret will Himself reward you openly."

Matthew 25:14-30—These scriptures talk about the parable of the talents, which basically teaches that we are to return to the Lord the increase of our work. For example, whatever investment returns we receive, whatever pay increases we are given, we are to return some portion to the Lord. These are financial examples, but this also applies to our spiritual giftings. All we are and have are to be used for God's glory.

Acts 5:1-11—These scriptures talk about the account of Ananias and Sapphira, who lied to the Holy Spirit about the amount they gave to the Lord's work and dropped dead due to their lying. We are never to lie to God and others about our giving or about anything.

1 Corinthians 16:1—"Concerning the collection for the saints…on the first day of the week let each one of you lay something aside, storing up as he may prosper."

2 Corinthians 8:10-15—These scriptures cover the purpose of giving: that there may be basic equality—that those who have abundance share with those who have little so every believer's needs are met.

2 Corinthians 9:7—"Let each one give as he purposes in his heart, not grudgingly or of necessity; for God loves a cheerful giver."

In the New Testament, there is not a Levitical law that demands a tenth of our wages, but the principle that each believer purposes in his heart what to give, and does it cheerfully without grumbling. A tenth, however, is a good, simple figure to start from, and God will lead you from there. Beware of selfish thinking regarding giving: God will not automatically increase our reward financially ten-fold, but He does promise blessings. He could give us increases in other ways, but the heart of our giving is not to get something back from God. It is recognizing that it is all His anyway, and we are just given stewardship over what He has given us.

God says, in 1 Timothy 5:17-18, to give double honor to the elders, "especially those who labor in the Word and doctrine. For the Scripture says…'the laborer is worthy of his wages.'" Clearly, we are to pay the church for those who labor, especially those who teach God's Word.

The heart of God is for us to purpose what to give right away, not basing our giving on what is left over at the end of the week. That way, He has our money and our money does not have us. God does not want us to be in bondage to our money but to exercise good stewardship. As we put Him first, we are free. There are consequences if we do not handle the money He has given us well but that is our fault, and not God's. Keep in mind that giving is not only about money but also giving of our time and gifts to the Body of Christ.

Let's assume that we are going to give a tenth of our income to the Lord's work. Do we tithe on our net (after tax) or on our gross (before tax) income? The Bible is silent on that account. It does say to "render to Caesar the things that are Caesar's, and to God the things that are God's" (Mark 12:17), but that does not answer the above question precisely. Those who advocate tithing on our after-tax dollars (net income), point out that the taxes paid to the government never come under our "stewardship control", so were never ours in the first place. Those advocating tithing on our pre-tax dollars tend to operate on the adjusted gross income which is that remaining after adding in interest while deducting business expenses, inventory, and losses. The important thing is that God wants us to be cheerful givers, each determining in his own heart what is right. So, pray about what you should give and study God's word regarding giving. You may be in a place where you would not be able to feed your family if you tithed, so do not let this burden you. God wants our heart, so make a commitment to some kind of giving plan with gradual increases as God enables and guides.

YEAR AT-A-GLANCE

The following two pages are to help you plan for your monthly bills and extra bills that come in approximately the same time each year and can help you plan your finances. Read the following, and then proceed with filling out the pages (or their equivalent, such as using a spreadsheet computer program).

On the page listed 12-MONTH FINANCIAL PLANNER for Routine Bills, list the monthly or every-other-month bills you pay. That includes credit cards, telephone, gas, electric, and rent or mortgage payments. In the months provided, write in the amount (or approximate amount) of the bill. Add each column to obtain a monthly total, and then add each monthly total to obtain a yearly total.

Next, take your yearly total and divide that number by the number of paychecks you receive per year. That number is the amount you are to put aside each paycheck to pay all your bills as they come in each month.

On the page listed 12-MONTH FINANCIAL PLANNER FOR EXTRA BILLS, list bills such as homeowner's insurance, car insurance, DMV, car maintenance approximation, real-estate taxes, subscriptions to magazines, health-club membership if not monthly, and any other bill that comes less than every two months.

In the months provided, write in the amount (or approximate amount) of the bill. Add each column to obtain a monthly total, and then add each monthly total to obtain a yearly total.

Next, take your yearly total and divide that by the number of paychecks you receive per year. That is the amount you are to put aside each paycheck to pay all your extra bills as they come in throughout the year. Some individuals set up a separate savings account for those bills, while others use envelopes in the home for the same purpose. Where you decide to keep extra money is best determined by whether you are tempted to spend it, if it is readily available. For instance, a four-month CD that is set aside every month for real-estate taxes cannot be touched until it matures. If you set it up to mature every March, August, and November, you have the money available to use in time to pay your two tax installments in April and December. If however, you think you can keep the extra money at home safely, you have the advantage of having the cash available should you need to borrow from it as long as you promptly pay the envelope back at your next paycheck. The goal is to be prepared and have the funds available to pay these bills in order to lessen chaos and stress in our lives.

YEAR AT-A-GLANCE---12-MONTH FINANCIAL PLANNER
FOR ROUTINE BILLS

Month	Gas	Water	Phone	Rent/ Mortgage	Medical Insurance	Life Insurance	Car Pmnt	Credit Card	Monthly Total
Jan.									
Feb.									
March									
April									
May									
June									
July									
August									
Sept.									
Oct.									
Nov.									
Dec.									

Yearly Total: _____

FORMULA: Yearly total divided by number of paychecks = amt. to save per paycheck.

Yearly total: _____   Amount to save per paycheck: _____

YEAR AT-A-GLANCE---12-MONTH FINANCIAL PLANNER
FOR EXTRA BILLS

Month	Car Insurance	Magazine subscription	Property Tax				Monthly Total
Jan.							
Feb.							
March							
April							
May							
June							
July							
August							
Sept.							
Oct.							
Nov.							
Dec.							

Yearly Total: _____

FORMULA: Yearly total divided by number of paychecks = amt. to save per paycheck.

Yearly total: _____   Amount to save per paycheck: _____

▲▲▲

DECISION MAKING/PROBLEM-SOLVING PROCESS

The below are the steps to support the making of informed decisions. Looking at the consequences of each of the choices to make when making decisions, prepares you to commit or not commit to that particular decision. While you may not always know future consequences, seeking wise counsel is a great tool to use to assist you in making decisions, regardless of the decision size.

Step 1
Determine the problem or decision facing you.

Step 2
Determine what is causing the problem.

Step 3
Consider your options from a biblical perspective. What alternative actions can you take?

Step 4
Determine the consequences to the options before you.

Step 5
Pray for wisdom and boldness in doing the will of God, seek godly counsel for important matters, and make a decision based on all the information you have available to you at the time.

Step 6
Act on your decision.

Step 7
Evaluate your decision.

Step 8
Modify the decision as needed. Rejoice if things work out well but if they don't, you need not regard your decision as a failure. Just learn from it, which is failing forward! Take responsibility for your own choices and do not blame others if what you desired does not occur. Make the Serenity Prayer your own when making tough decisions: "God, grant me the serenity to accept the things I cannot change, the courage to change the things I can, and the wisdom to know the difference."

TIME TO PRACTICE!

Now that you have the steps, it is time to practice!

What is the problem?

_____

What is causing the problem?

_____

_____

What alternative actions can you take?

Option 1:

_____

_____

Option 2:

_____

_____

Option 3:

_____

_____

What consequences will happen with each of the above options?

Option 1--consequences:

_____

_____

Option 2--consequences:

_____

_____

Option 3--consequences:

_____

_____

Most of us have been taught to think in black and white, with usually only one right decision to make. We often fail to look at ALL the factors inherent in a situation before deciding on a course of action. Many times we just react. Exploring all the avenues of action God gives us for addressing decisions/problems will keep us from unnecessarily boxing ourselves in. It frees us to work cooperatively and collaboratively with others.

The course of action you have decided on is:

_____

_____

The result of my action was:

_____

_____

I need to change my decision in the following way:

_____

_____

I have learned the following about the decision-making process:

_____

_____

▲ ▲ ▲

LIFE PHILOSOPHY

After Life Philosophy is a section on Goal Setting. To set goals, you first get to dig deep and discover your Life Philosophy: That which directs and guides you daily; your fundamental beliefs.

You have a philosophy of life whether you think you do or not. It can be seen in how you spend your time and money, what you view is important, and what you want to do with your life. All too often, we do not do what we view or say is important and don't accomplish what we want to do with our lives because we have not reflected on these important things. Most of the time we don't write down what's important to us. We don't allow our own eyes to see nor do we seek to do what's important to us. We take on what society or others view as important and life flies by, not being truly lived according to the destiny ordained for each of us by our Creator. PLEASE STOP and don't let that be you!

The following are elements that you get to evaluate prior to writing your own lifephilosophy:

ELEMENTS:

1. My values are: (the bottom line of a philosophy)
2. My beliefs about the world, life, and universe are:
3. What I want to accomplish or live out:
4. How I intend to accomplish the above:

In the spaces provided below, write what you believe to be true today under each category.

1. MY VALUES:

_____

_____

_____

_____

_____

2. MY BELIEFS ABOUT THE WORLD, LIFE AND UNIVERSE:

_____

_____

_____

_____

3. WHAT I WANT TO ACCOMPLISH OR LIVE OUT:

_____

_____

_____

_____

_____

4. HOW I INTEND TO ACCOMPLISH THE ABOVE:

_____

_____

_____

_____

_____

LIFE PHILOSOPHY EXAMPLE
Written 1992, revised 2007

I believe that God created all things. I believe that Jesus won the battle over Satan when He died on the cross and rose from the dead, with the resultant breaking of the bondage to sin for those who believe.

Because of this belief, I will to live my life under God's protection and provision and live as His Spirit teaches me; in power, freedom, and joy as His child—a child of the King, called to excellence as his ambassador, not perfection. Only He is perfect.

I want my life to show:

- That I care for people above all else.
- Joy, peace and freedom.
- Depth of character.

I will accomplish what I want my life to show by: (the values listed in the book, The Travelers Gift [TG], are included in the parentheses).

- Accepting the responsibility for my choices and life, and that what happens or doesn't happen, is up to me. (TG—living by choice and responsibility, decided heart, forgiveness, no blame game, and the buck stops here)
- Training myself to stop and actively listen when others speak. (TG—humble, seeking wisdom, caring and loving)
- Staying repentant and having an attitude of, "not my will but Yours be done." (TG—submitted, humble, thinking of others before myself)
- Accept beneficial as well as adverse circumstances, knowing that what touches me is only what has been allowed by my Creator and Father. (TG—surrender and acceptance which fosters joy and gratefulness)
- Seeking to learn from the error of my ways. (TG—humility and failing forward, persevering without exception)
- Enjoying and rejoicing in what God originally gave us to rule and subdue. (Genesis 1:28 and fighting in the front lines in my spiritual armor [Ephesians 6:10-19] against the enemy of our souls. (TG—choosing and responsible to act, active, giving, pouring out, bold, tough love, powerful, passionate, committed, and living with intention)
- Studying and obeying God's Word first and foremost. (TG—the Truth, a decided heart)

Use this page to write out your own life's philosophy and obviously, without the Traveler's Gift values listed, unless you have read this book. Eloquence is not necessary as this is only for you. Review it occasionally and revise as needed.

▲ ▲ ▲

My Life Philosophy
Date:

GOAL SETTING

Many individuals have never been taught about goal setting. This exercise will teach you how to clearly state your goals and then set up sub-goals (activities) to achieve your stated goal/s.

First—why should we set goals? Isn't God supposed to do everything for us? He can move me, can't He? So, why do I have to do anything?

Yes, God can move us if He so desires to work that way. Most often, He doesn't. He can speak to us, but it is up to us to take action as His vessels here on earth. Setting goals can be for any part of our life—for what God has spoken to us to do, for our own growth, for our education, or for fun. When goals are set, a purpose grows within us. We are not just skimming along in life doing who knows what. The goal does not have to be some great feat, but as we begin setting goals and moving forward, God directs our path. You can direct a moving car, but not a parked car. Goals help us get moving!

Think of the term SMARTER to support you in setting up your goals:

S: simple yet specific

M: measurable

A: achievable

R: realistic

T: timely

E: evaluate

R: reset goal

The S is self-explanatory. The M means that you can measure the behavior. A means you will be able to accomplish the goal, and goes along with R, which means that the goal is not too highly set. If a goal is too highly set, we set ourselves up to fail. The T means the goal is to be done within a reasonable time frame, with an end stated in the goal. When the end is achieved, the goal can be reset again or changed. The E is for us to determine if we achieved the goal or not, and why. Was the goal really important to us? What could we have done differently to achieve what we set out to do? Was the goal too highly set (as often happens in weight reduction)? Once the evaluation phase is done, the goal can be discarded or reset, which is what the R stands for.

Sample Goal:

I will study my Bible 4 times a week for 1 hour over one-month, in June.

      S: Personal Bible study
      M: 4 times / week
      A: clearly stated
      R: can be achieved
      T: over a month's time (specify which month)
      E: needs to be done after a month's time or throughout the month
      R: select another month or pick different Bible-study goals

Sub-goals are those behaviors or specific activities we must do to achieve our expected end. In the example above, that might involve setting the alarm earlier, choose the place and time for Bible study, not planning anything else for that time period, and turning our phones off. We can be as creative as we need to be.

On the following pages, write down some goals that you want to incorporate in your life and the sub-goals or activities needed to achieve them.

LIFE DOMAIN GOALS

Life Domains (adjust the following to your needs)

SPIRITUAL GOALS: Activities:

_____   _____

_____   _____

_____   _____

_____   _____

HEALTH AND FITNESS: Activities:

_____   _____

_____   _____

_____   _____

_____   _____

JOB: Activities:

_____   _____

_____   _____

_____   _____

_____   _____

EDUCATION: Activities:

_____   _____

_____   _____

_____   _____

_____   _____

SOCIAL/FAMILY: Activities:

_____   _____

_____   _____

_____   _____

_____   _____

RECREATION: Activities:

_____   _____

_____   _____

_____   _____

FINANCIAL: Activities:

_____   _____

_____   _____

_____   _____

List an area of your life and state where you see God leading you in that area within the next year, 5 years, and 10 years. You can repeat this with any area of your life. If you do not have any direction right now, seek the Lord and begin to make plans but be ever watchful in case you are going off His path for you. He will let you know, and guide you as you move out. Proverbs 16:9 states, "A man's heart plans his way, but the Lord directs his steps." Proverb 16:3 promises, that when you "commit your works to the Lord, your thoughts will be established." How wonderful to know that He will give us clear and solid thoughts as we trust and obey Him!

Area:

_____

1 year:

_____

5 years:

_____

10 years:

_____

▲ ▲ ▲

THE GRIEF PROCESS

How do we respond to the loss of a dearly loved person or object? The difficulty in overcoming the effects of grief depends on the nature and depth of the loss, our support systems, and our ability to feel our sorrow. To feel grief after a significant loss is normal, natural, and to be expected. When people experience loss, they grieve. We can grieve even for what we did not have, such as growing up without our father or mother, and then beginning to realize how much we missed their not being around for us.

Grief process—as defined by Dr. Elisabeth Kübler-Ross. (1960). On Death & Dying. Simon & Schuster-Touchstone. Dr. Ross did extensive research on grieving families.

1. Denial
   a. No, I don't want to believe it. It can't be!
   b. Numbness and shock.
2. Anger
   a. Directed at self or another.
   b. Irritability with mood swings over small things.
   c. Guilt feelings: What did I do wrong?
   d. Wanting to hurt the one who left us.
3. Bargaining
   a. God, if I do this, will you cause that to happen?
   b. Please, God: I'll do better if you change _____.
4. Depression
   a. Emptiness, loss of meaning, sadness, sorrow.
   b. Forgetfulness, aimless wandering, inability to concentrate.
   c. Overeating, undereating.
   d. Crying often and unexpectedly.
   e. Physical complaints.
   f. Isolation, apathy, loneliness.
   g. Feelings of losing control.
   h. Anxiety about the future.
5. Acceptance
   a. Hope comes through.
   b. We affirm the reality of our new situation.
   c. Fear leaves.
   d. We start to move forward again.

Grieving is a process we get to allow ourselves to go through in order to get past our pain. Each person's passage through grief differs, but if the shock and or denial phase continues for weeks, the person may need professional assistance to move forward and begin facing reality.

No one goes through the grieving process perfectly from stages 1-5. We can bounce back and forth between stages, dealing with issues until we are done. We can get to the acceptance stage and then leave it briefly. The important thing is to provide and allow time to feel and grieve; trusting in God to move us along. In our culture, we are not taught how to grieve or how to support others who grieve. Most individuals try "Band-Aid therapy," which is well meant but causes isolation and gives the message that the person should not feel what they are feeling. It sounds like this: "Why are you crying? Don't you know you need faith in God?"; "OK, time to get moving again." Use the following to allow the grieving process to take place at a healthy pace.

DO'S	DON'TS
Be available to listen, not give unwanted advice.	Don't avoid your grieving friend.
Do encourage others to be patient with themselves.	Don't say how they should feel.
Do be available to run errands or just spend time with them.	Don't say you know how they feel.
Allow others to express as much grief as they are feeling and are willing to share.	Don't say that they should be grateful for what happened.
	Don't say, "You should be feeling better by now." Instead, ask how you can support them and pray often.

Jesus grieved. As He was entering Jerusalem, He wept over the city (Luke 19:41). Before His arrest in the garden of Gethsemane, Jesus said to His disciples, "My soul is exceedingly sorrowful, even to death. Stay here and watch with Me." (Matthew 26:38) Luke 22:44 tells us that, "being in agony, He prayed more earnestly. Then His sweat became like great drops of blood falling down to the ground." Jesus had emotions and took them all to God. He had grief so heavy it was almost death inside to Him.

He can relate to us, and is our example in how to handle our grief. Hopefully, our friends will not be as the disciples were, who slept when Jesus asked for companionship. No matter what, know that Jesus sympathizes with our weaknesses and grief, for He "was in all points tempted as we are, yet without sin. Let us therefore come boldly to the throne of grace that we may obtain mercy and find grace to help in time of need" (Hebrews 4:15-16; cf. Hebrews 2: 14-18).

THE FIRST AND SECOND GREATEST COMMANDMENTS

Loving One Another As Ourselves

In Matthew 22:36-40 we find a great answer to a truly great question. The question is, "Which is the great commandment in the law?" Jesus' profound answer is "'You shall love the Lord your God with all your heart...soul, and...mind.' This is the first and greatest commandment. And the second is like it: 'You shall love your neighbor as yourself.' On these two commandments hang all the Law and the Prophets."

What is this love all about? First, we must receive God's mercy for ourselves and then extend it to others. As we evaluate ourselves honestly before God, we begin to see our sinfulness. Acknowledging and repenting of our sinfulness before God and receiving His forgiveness through Christ puts us in a right relationship with Him. He then begins to change us. As we see how sinful we are before the Holy One and receive His mercy (no condemnation with repentance), we can better understand others and extend to them the mercy we received (the love really extends from God).

Loving one another also includes chastising and reproving another. As God's holy Force convicts us and holds us accountable to Him, so we are to be accountable to others and receive their reproof as well as reprove them. That does not give us the liberty to open our mouths and speak without loving discernment. Rather, this is a <u>HEAVY RESPONSIBILITY</u> to act in love and not condemnation towards others—to hate the sin, but love the sinner. Personal attacks are not allowed in God's family, which grows together in all the frailties of our human nature. As we live together as a family, we become aware of each other's shortcomings. As that happens, first pray: Pray for the person, and ask God if He desires words to be spoken. Be careful and let wisdom and caution be your guide since damage is easily done but not easily repaired. If in doubt, ask for godly guidance.

THE TEN COMMANDMENTS

The following are the Ten Commandments given by God in Exodus 20 and repeated in Deuteronomy 5. Many individuals have never read them, though they have heard of them. Echoing the two greatest commandments summarized by Jesus, notice that the first four commandments teach us how to love God, and the last six, how to love others.

Commandment 1:

"I am the Lord your God... You shall have no other gods before Me."

Worship only our creator, who is one God, yet three distinct Persons: God the Father, God the Son, and God the Holy Spirit.

Commandment 2:

"You shall not make for yourself a carved image. You shall not bow down to them, nor serve them. For I, the Lord your God, am a jealous God."

Do not worship things. Worship God alone.

Commandment 3:

"You shall not take the name of the Lord your God in vain."

Never use God's name as a swear word, or make fun of holy things.

Commandment 4:

"Remember the Sabbath day; to keep it holy."

Keep God's day special and use it for Him.

Commandment 5:

"Honor your father and your mother, that your days may be long, and that it may be well with you."

Love and obey your parents.

Commandment 6:

"You shall not murder."

Because man is made in God's image, never take a life unless absolutely necessary.

Commandment 7:

"You shall not commit adultery."

Do not take another person's husband or wife.

Commandment 8:

"You shall not steal."

Respect the property of others.

Commandment 9:

"You shall not bear false witness against your neighbor."

Do not lie about anyone.

Commandment 10:

"You shall not covet your neighbor's wife; and you shall not desire your neighbor's house, his field, or anything that is your neighbor's."

Do not want what belongs to others (a heart attitude of coveting).

MY PRAISE SONG

My pain is real. It hurts. At times, I feel as if I am dead inside. Other times I feel as if my heart is breaking into pieces. But—I have come to appreciate my pain for what it teaches me.

I feel solid inside when I acknowledge my pain, which is a special feeling for me. Far too often in the past, I have been tossed to and fro, not wanting to feel my sorrow. I cheated myself of feeling the depth to which my pain goes.

BUT NO MORE

I grow as I experience and listen to my pain. Movement happens within me without my even trying to make it happen. My path becomes clearer before me as I walk with my pain rather than around it.

BUT THERE IS MORE

I have learned that without knowing my pain and sorrow, I cannot fully appreciate and experience the joy that is within me. I have also come to see that as I acknowledge all that is within me, I am experiencing life and living the woman GOD made me to be. When I die, I will know that I have lived life to the fullest: That I have loved well, cried well, and have lived fully human, fully alive.

THIS IS MY PRAISE SONG.

©nw

I want to acknowledge John Powell's book, Fully Human, Fully Alive,
for impacting and inspiring me at a young age.

▲ ▲ ▲

THE WAY IT IS MEANT TO BE

Free from worry,
Free from fear,
Trusting You.

-THIS IS THE WAY-

Separate to You alone,
Living out what was ordained for me,
For why else should I be here?

-THIS IS THE WAY-

Sharing myself with others but
Not losing myself to them in the process,
For I belong to You alone.

-THIS IS THE WAY-

Receiving from others,
Loving them deeply with all my being, but
Knowing that they belong to You alone.

-THIS IS THE WAY-

Free to fly to the music of Your joy,
Free to enjoy Your earth with thanks and praises,
Free to feel Your wind blowing through my hair,
Free to feel Your waves tumble me in playfulness,
Free to experience others in separateness.

FREE CHOICE _____

-THE WAY IT IS MEANT TO BE-

©nw

⩓ ⩓ ⩓

DEAR LITTLE ONE,

I made you. I love you. Yet you struggle so hard. All around you are voices and messages that say you are no good. I tell you this: They are lying. Do not believe them. When I knit you together in your mother's womb, I used the pattern that was just for you. I used it for no one else. Continue fighting. You must believe what I tell you. I will never lie to you.

You are the person you are supposed to be. You do not have to try to be someone else to be loved by Me. Others may try to tell you that you do. Remember: Do not believe them! You can only be who I made you to be. You cannot be anyone else. It is all I ask of you regarding this. But I do ask you not to be less than I have made you. Be true to yourself, and in so doing you will be true to Me. You will please Me.

I love you. I know it is hard and your pain is great. I understand that. But know the pain will be greater if you try to change who I made you to be, not less.

My child, listen to those whose words and acts prove they love you. Do not believe the others. But most of all, listen to Me. For I love you beyond all others. I love you the way I made you. Be that person and love yourself in My Name.

Anonymous

▲ ▲ ▲

SERENITY PRAYER

The serenity prayer is included here, as it points towards dependence upon God, which is what He wants from us. There are great benefits to memorizing this, as God's holy Force will bring it to your remembrance when you need it the most!

God, grant me the serenity to accept the things I cannot change, the courage to change the things that I can, and the wisdom to know the difference.

God, grant me the serenity to accept the things I cannot change.

List of things I cannot change:

_____

_____

_____

_____

God, grant me the courage to change the things that I can.

List of things I can change:

_____

_____

_____

God, grant me the wisdom to know the difference.

How I can tell the difference between the two:

_____

_____

_____

▲ ▲ ▲

COME, CHILD OF MY LOVE

Come and rest in me. Rest, knowing you are My beloved, the apple of My eye. I am right by your side. Never have I been closer, never have I loved you more.

Remember, all that I do, I do in deep abiding love. I am a wise husbandman, seeing the end from the beginning, and have purposes of untold love for you and your loved ones.

I called you and choose you from your mother's womb. I have a special plan for your life. You are a chosen vessel of honor; I have set you apart for My special purposes.

Do your nerves wince from a heavy blow that has come upon you? Do not fear: It is shaping you, producing radiance from a precious jewel. I am teaching you the patience of faith, the courage of faith, and the victory of faith. Know for sure, precious one, that I am working on your behalf and on behalf of each of your loved ones.

Do you feel crushed under a heavy load? Do you feel you've been broken and lay in useless pieces? Then rejoice and remember it is the broken clay I dwell in most richly. When you are at the end of your strength and wisdom, then I am free to work mightily on your behalf. If you are broken, do not despair: I will use you for My glory. Joseph was broken in Egypt's prison and was prepared for a crown. Moses was broken in the wilderness and led My people free from Egypt's bondage! It is the broken I use most.

Let patience have her perfect work in this hard place. Your times are in My hand. Do not steal tomorrow out of My hands. Learn to wait on Me. Do not let delays dishearten you, for I am bringing about My perfect will in all of this. In quietness and rest is your strength. Remember, My ways are perfect. You have given Me your life as a sacred trust, and I have received it as such.

Commit your way to Me and I will bring it to pass. No work or plan of Mine can be hindered. You have sought My Kingdom and My will and that you shall have. No matter how things appear, know that I am working all things to the good of those who love Me! I shall have the glory!

Come, I will carry you—rest in My arms. Do not faint in the day of adversity, for I am your refuge and strength in desperate hours. I will never fail you and you will not fail Me.

Come, rest in my arms. Lay your head upon My breast, trusting in My love and wisdom. I have held nothing back of My love. Since I offered up My precious Son, Jesus, how much more will I help you now?

Wait, hope, trust, and believe in Me, child of My love!

Anonymous

⋏ ⋏ ⋏

BIBLIOGRAPHY

Andrews, Andy. (2002). The Traveler's Gift. Tennessee: Thomas Nelson, Inc.

Beattie, Melody. (1987). Codependent No More. New York: Harper & Row.

Bender, Stephanie & Keleher, Kathleen. (1991). PMS—A Positive Program to Gain Control. New York: The Body Press.

Bennett, Dennis & Rita. (1971). The Holy Spirit and You. New Jersey: Logos International.

Berkhof, Louis. (1933). Manual of Christian Doctrine. Michigan: William B. Eerdmans Publishing Company.

Bradshaw, John. (1988). The Family. Florida: Health Communications, Inc.

Bridges, Jerry. (1978). The Pursuit of Holiness. Colorado: Navpress.

Bridges, Jerry. (1983). The Practice of Godliness. Colorado: Navpress.

Buhler, Rich. (1988). Pain and Pretending. Tennessee: Thomas Nelson, Inc.

Burkett, Larry. (1990). The Financial Planning Workbook. Chicago: Moody Press.

Campbell, Roderick. (1954). Israel and the New Covenant. Pennsylvania: Presbyterian and Reformed Publishing Company.

Cloud, H., & Townsend, J. (1992). Boundaries. Michigan: Zondervan Publishing House.

Corey, Gerald F. (1977). Theory and Practice of Counseling and Psychotherapy (2nd ed.). California: Wadsworth.

Dileo, Sandy. (1984). "Stress Management". California: Author.

Edman, V. Raymond. (1948). The Disciplines of Life. Minnesota: World Wide Publication.

Elwell, Walter A. (Editor). (1989). Evangelical Commentary on the Bible. Michigan: Baker Book House.

Engstrom, Ted W. (1976). The Making of a Christian Leader. Michigan: Zondervan Publishing House.

Erickson, Millard J. (1985). Christian Theology. Michigan: Baker Book House.

Esses, Michael. (1974). The Phenomenon of Obedience. New Jersey: Logos International.

Foster, Richard. (1992). Prayer—Finding the Heart's True Home. California: Harper.

Fromm, Erich. (1956). The Art of Loving. New York: Harper & Row.

Green, Michael. (1975). I Believe in the Holy Spirit. Michigan: Wm. B. Eerdmans Publishing Company.

Hammond, Frank & Ida. (1973). Pigs In The Parlor. Missouri: Impact Books.

Hart, S.L. (1968). Lifetime of Love. Mass: Daughters of St. Paul.

Johnson, Spencer, MD. (1998). Who Moved My Cheese? USA: Penguin Group.

Lancaster, Wade & Jeanette. (1982). "Rational Decision Making: Managing Uncertainty". Journal of Nursing Administration. Sept. 1982. pgs. 23-28.

Leman, Dr. Kevin. (1981). Sex Begins in the Kitchen. California: Regal Books.

MacNutt, Francis, O.P. (1974). Healing. Indiana: Ave Maria Press.

Martin, Dr. Walter. (1962). Essential Christianity. California: GL Publications.

Martin, Francis P. (1979). Hung by the Tongue. Louisiana: F.P.M. Publications.

McAll, Dr. Kenneth. (1982). Healing the Family Tree. Great Britain: Sheldon Press.

Moody, Dwight L. (1881). Secret Power. California: Regal Books.

Murphy, Dr. Ed. (1992). The Handbook for Spiritual Warfare. Tennessee: Thomas Nelson Publishers, Inc.

Nutrition Search, Inc. (1973). Nutrition Almanac. New York: McGraw-Hill Book Company.

Payne, Leanne. (1991). Restoring the Christian Soul Through Healing Prayer. Illinois: Crossway Books.

Peck, M. Scott, MD. (1978). The Road Less Traveled. New York: Simon & Schuster, Inc.

Peck, M. Scott, MD. (1983). People of the Lie. New York: Simon & Schuster, Inc.

Penner, Clifford & Joyce. (1981). The Gift of Sex. Texas: Word, Inc.

Powell, John. (1969). Why Am I Afraid to Tell You Who I Am?. Illinois: Argus Communications.

Powell, John. (1974). The Secret of Staying in Love. Texas: Argus Communications.

Powell, John. (1976). Fully Human, Fully Alive. Illinois: Argus Communications.

Powell, John. (1978). Unconditional Love. Texas: Argus Communications.

Ross, Elisabeth Kübler-. (1960). On Death & Dying. Simon & Schuster/Touchstone.

Sanders, J. Oswald. (1967). Spiritual Leadership. Illinois: Moody Bible Institute.

Schaeffer, Francis A. (1971). True Spirituality. Illinois: Tyndale House Publishers.

Seamands, David A. (1981). Healing for Damaged Emotions. Illinois: SP Publications, Inc.

Smalley, Gary & Trent, John, Ph.D. (1986). The Blessing. Tennessee: Thomas Nelson, Inc.

Smalley, Gary & Trent, John, Ph.D. (1988). The Language of Love. California: Focus on the Family.

Smalley, Gary & Trent, John, Ph.D. (1990). The Two Sides of Love. Colorado: Focus on the Family.

Smith, Chuck. (1980). Effective Prayer Life. California: The Word for Today.

Swindoll, Charles R. (1983). Dropping Your Guard. New York: Bantam Books.

Taylor, Richard Shelley. (1962). The Disciplined Life. Minnesota: Bethany House Publishers.

Torrey, R.A. (1974 revised edition). The Person & Work of the Holy Spirit. Michigan: Zondervan Publishing House.

Vine, W. E. (1981). Vine's Expository Dictionary of Old and New Testament Words. New Jersey: Fleming H. Revell Company.

Watson, David. (1980). The Hidden Battle. Illinois: Harold Shaw Publishers.

White, Tom. (1993). Breaking Strongholds: How Spiritual Warfare Sets Captives Free. Michigan: Servant Publications.

Whitfield, Charles L., M.D. (1987). Healing the Child Within. Florida: Health Communications, Inc.

Wilkerson, David & Sherrill, John & Elizabeth. (1963). The Cross and The Switchblade. New Jersey: Spire Books.

Wilkerson, David. (1972). The Pocket Promise Book. California: Regal Books.

Williams, Dr. Roger J. (1971). Nutrition Against Disease. New York: Pitman Publishing Corporation.

Made in the USA
San Bernardino, CA
12 September 2016